IN SEARCH OF
HIGHER GROUND

To my wife Laura and my children Grace and Aidan.
Thank you for inspiring me to reach for Higher Ground
and for keeping my feet on Solid Ground.

I love you

CONTENTS

WHAT IS HIGHER GROUND?

What is Higher Ground? It is anything that is good and positive that you desire for your life. It may mean financial freedom, early retirement or the ownership of personal property. It could mean the beginning of a business that up to this point has only been a dream. Higher Ground may be the corporate ladder that is waiting for you to climb, the book that is waiting to be written, the idea that is waiting to become reality. It could mean a better way of life, a healthier marriage or successful parenting. It may be freedom from an addiction or an overcoming of a past hurt that continues to damage the future. Simply put, Higher Ground is the place where you live out your dreams.

Higher Ground is different for everyone...it's path is different, the obstacles vary, the surroundings rarely look the same. Although it varies in size, shape and color what it takes to get to Higher Ground is most often the same. Dreams, Goals, Risk taking, letting go of fear and insecurity, character, mental attitude, right motives, accountability, these are all things you must have placed in your backpack as you journey up the mountain to this place called Higher Ground.

Many years ago I was invited to go on a long backpacking trip. For those who know me well I am not much of a outdoors person. My idea of the outdoors is laying by the pool at the Marriott. I was told to be a part of this backpacking trip, I would have to attend an orientation meeting in which we would receive instruction on what to bring and how to prepare. Beyond my better judgement I attended this meeting and received the information. The guide for the trip had divided up the list of who would bring what. Each person was assigned various tasks and duties to help make the trip a success. I purchased all the items I was assigned and in a few short days I found myself on a week long back packing trip that I will never forget.

We drove all night to the mountain we were to climb until finally we arrived. With very little sleep we began to climb the mountain. For the next 8 hours all we did was climb. The guide and the few who had been on a trip like this were doing fine. Myself and the others who had never been on a backpacking adventure felt like we were dying. Finally after hours of climbing and complaining we arrived at a sight where we unpacked, got cleaned up and had an opportunity to eat. Even though it wasn't very comfortable we all slept like babies through the night.

The next morning, however, the guide woke us up and told us it was time to pack up and continue the climb up the mountain. I had honestly thought that we had arrived the day before, that we were not going to climb anymore. I tried to reason with the guide, I told him what is the difference between staying here and climbing higher. The trees look the same, the ground looks the same, what could possibly be different by climbing the mountain any higher. After much pleading, complaining, whining and anything else I could do to change his mind, we moved on. We continued to climb all day until we arrived to our final destination at just about sunset. I was so tired that after eating and getting cleaned up, I went immediately to sleep. The next morning I awoke and realized that we were at the top of the mountain. The guide was absolutely right. The trees looked different,

WITHOUT A DREAM LIFE BECOMES SOMETHING TO BE ENDURED NOT ENJOYED.

the air was cleaner, the surrounding was only something I had seen on a postcard. I realized something that morning that I will never forget, that the view is always better at the top of the mountain. That somehow you forget all the work that it took to get you there when you finally arrive at Higher Ground!

The first characteristic to reaching Higher Ground is found in this story of my mountain top experience. You see, the difference between me and the guide was that he had been to the top and I had not. He had a picture in his mind of what it looked like and I had never seen it. The mountain top was a place he loved, a passion he had, a dream that so captured his thoughts that fatigue would not and could not stand in the way.

You see, that's the power of a dream. It becomes your compass, your passion, your love, your guide and your thoughts. Dreams become a sense of purpose and direction for where your life is headed. Without a dream life becomes something to be endured not enjoyed. It becomes something where we get by, but not get ahead.

Jim Marshall has been described as the most indestructible man ever to play professional football. In a sport where thirty is considered old age, he played defensive end until he was forty-two, starting in 282 consecutive games. He is what famous quarterback Fran Tarkenton called "the most amazing athlete I've ever known in any sport."

Jim, however, has had his share of struggles. He's suffered a gunshot wound, had been sick with pneumonia twice, has been in several automobile accidents, has undergone dramatic surgery and once was caught in a blizzard in which all his friends that were with him died. Jim understands what it means to face trials. The secret of Jim's amazing success is in his two guidelines: Find a direction and dedicate yourself to it and remember that you can go as far as you want to go if you have a dream. Jim has realized the power of a dream and more importantly he lived it out.

The first step towards Higher Ground is knowing your dream and being committed to it. Take a look at the four ways that will help you to clarify your dreams and get you moving towards fulfilling them:

❶ DREAM WITHOUT RESERVATION

In other words don't be afraid to dream! Dream big, it doesn't cost anything, it doesn't hurt you, it doesn't damage you emotionally. It won't abandon you or reject you, or do anything harmful to you. Dreams are wonderful! They are a blank page in which to write out your deepest thoughts. There a canvass of potential in which all that is possible is laid out for you to envision.

Often what keeps us from dreaming is the fear of what others may think of our dream. Will they think it's foolish, will they think I'm out of my mind or maybe they'll laugh at me when I tell them my dreams and aspirations for the future.

"IF YOU DON'T HAVE A FEW PEOPLE LAUGHING AT YOUR DREAMS, IT MAY JUST MEAN YOUR NOT DREAMING BIG ENOUGH."

Can you imagine what people thought of the Wright Brothers when they spoke of building a craft that would carry human beings and allow them to soar above the earth? What a crazy idea people must have thought. It was reported that people thought a human body could not handle the speed or the altitude. The critics lined up to take pop shots at them. But it was their dream, not the critics'. It was birthed inside of them and became a passion in their hearts. The passion grew stronger than the critics and thankfully for us the Wright Brothers dreamed bigger than others thought was possible.

The point is that you will have critics. But I have noticed in my life that those who are good at criticizing are rarely good at anything else. Critics are not dreamers, they simply tear down the dreams of others to a level that is comfortable for themselves. By tearing down the dream it releases them of the responsibility to live their lives at a higher level. Critics will always be there...but remember in the end criticism always discredits the critic. Dale Galloway in his book "Leading with Vision" said "If you don't have a few people laughing at your dreams, it may just mean your not dreaming big enough." So be a dreamer and dream big!!

❷ PUT YOUR DREAMS IN WRITING

Less then 5% of people ever put their dreams and visions for the future in writing. I don't know what it is about putting your dreams in writing but it just seems to help. I heard motivational speaker Anthony Robbins once say "There is something magical about putting your dreams in writing, they just seem to have a greater chance of becoming reality." I believe that. I have seen it work in my life and I have seen it work in the hundreds of lives that I have personally worked with.

In my family I have one brother. He had struggled with a drug addiction for years. When he finally decided to clean up his life, he came to stay with my wife and I for awhile. The first thing I had him do was to write out his dreams. To paint a picture of how he wanted his life to look 3 years from now. His list included: a steady job, a wife to love, a checking account (which he had never had) being drug free, repairing the damage on his teeth that had been done from his substance abuse and a few others. Three years after he wrote those dreams down nearly everyone of them came true. There is just something simply magical about writing them down.

> IT HAS BEEN SAID THAT IF YOU DON'T PLAN, THEN YOU ARE PLANNING TO FAIL.

John Goddard dared to dream. At the young age of fifteen he made a list of all the things he wanted to do in his life. That list contained 127 goals he hoped to achieve. It included such things as: explore the Nile, climb Mt. Everest, study primitive tribes in the Sudan, run a five minute mile, read the Bible from cover to cover, dive in a submarine, play "Claire de Lune" on the piano, write a book, read the entire Encyclopedia Britannica and circumnavigate the globe.

It has been reported that John Goddard has reached 105 of his 127 goals. He is still looking forward to visiting all 141 countries in the world (so far he has visited 113), exploring the entire Yangtze River in China and visiting the moon. John Goddard has experienced more then most people would in five lifetimes. But it all started at age fifteen when he put his dreams to ink.

I challenge you to do that. Put your dreams on paper. Taking dreams and writing them down is the beginning step to charting a course for success. It's taking them out of your head and heart and putting them down on paper that allows your dream to move from emotional to physical, from something you feel to something you can begin to see.

❸ MAKE A PLAN FOR YOUR DREAMS

Probably the biggest mistake people make is not planning. It has been said that if you don't plan, then you are planning to fail. I speak to people every week of the year and have the opportunity to meet a variety of individuals and I often hear people tell me of their dreams. "I want to be financially free, own a bigger home, start a business, learn an instrument, write a book" and many other dreams that are good and positive. My first question to them is "How?" How do you plan on getting this done! Quite often they are unsure of their plan to get this dream of theirs accomplished.

When a football team sets out to win a championship, that is a dream but what helps that dream come true is the carrying out of a plan. When an Olympic hopeful says "Someday I will stand on the platform with my country's flag waving behind me and gold around my neck" that is a dream. But only a plan will make that dream come true. When a high school graduate fantasizes about receiving a doctorate in his or her choice of study, that is a dream several years away. Unless there is a plan that is put into place, that student's dream will remain a dream for the rest of his life.

Dreams are a wonderful thing, but the point of a dream is that at some place in your life that dream will come true. Putting a plan together is what will fuel a dream to reality.

I have several dreams for my life. One of those dreams was to successfully plant a church in Corona, CA. So I sat down and I put my dreams to ink and then I created a plan. It included: funding, building a team, mission statements, core values, timelines, promotional plans. I not only placed on paper what I needed, but the steps necessary to see them accomplished. The task of planting a church is a difficult one, but having a plan to follow makes it a whole lot easier. My plans became the blueprints and all I needed to do was follow the outline.

LET ME GIVE YOU A QUICK PLAN ON HOW TO PUT YOUR DREAMS TO WORK:

a. **Dream Clarification:** What is the dream or goal that you would like to accomplish? Let's use an example and say that you wanted to learn a second language. The first thing you want to do is take a blank piece of paper and write at the top

"Learning a second language."

b. Assessment: Where are you now?   What are the resources you have to accomplish the goal of a second language? Do you know someone who can teach you? Do you have the finances to pay for instructions?   Write the resources down.

c. Goal setting: When do you want to have this accomplished? Put on your piece of paper a date in which you will have learned this second language.

d. Implementation: How do you plan on getting there? After you have considered your resources and the deadline you have set, you must now lay out a step by step plan to accomplish the goal. Try to break it down into a few steps so you don't get so overwhelmed. Also, put a date next to each step so you can measure whether or not you are on track to accomplish your goal.

e. Evaluation: When the deadline arrives, go back to your paper and evaluate whether or not you hit the goal. If you hit the goal, congratulate yourself. If you came up short, figure out why.

This simple method will work with any dream. Starting a business, buying a house or whatever your goal may be. However you choose to plan out your dreams is up to you, but whatever you do plan them out. Create a footprint to follow. It was Dr. Robert Schuller who once said "Yard by yard, life is hard, but inch by inch, it's a cinch."

❹ BE COMMITTED TO DOING WHATEVER IT TAKES

We are a society who is great at starting things. We start diets that we never finish, sign up at gyms we never attend, make commitments we don't follow through with. Many have made the long walk to the altar to say "I do" but then "never did." We are a society that follows through with very little. I have learned throughout the years that character is not only made in crisis, but it is also displayed in crisis. That the true character of an individual is not what they start, but what they finish. Anyone can start a marathon but it takes stamina to finish it. Anyone can set out to swim the English Channel but it takes endurance to complete it.

Dreams, goals and plans must be supported by the attitude of the dreamer that says, "I will do whatever it takes to make this happen. It may pull me out of my comfort zone or force me to change, but I will do whatever it takes to make it happen." This attitude must be taken on by those who dare to dream. Consider the discouragement these people must have faced...

- *"You're foolish to try to sell sparkling water in the land of Coca-Cola drinkers."* (advice given to Gustave Leven by a consulting firm about his idea to bring Perrier to the U.S.)

- *"You have a nice voice, but it's nothing special."* (Voice teacher about Diana Ross)

- *"You're fired from this newspaper because of a lack of creativity."* (told to Walt Disney)

- *"How long will you go on training all day in a gymnasium and living in a dream world?"* (families plea to get a 'respectable' job to Arnold Schwarzenegger)

- *"It's a cutthroat business and you've got no chance of success."* (accountant for Estee Lauder)

These are just a few people that had to work past criticism, obstacles, hard times, financial hardship and many other trials that can face a dreamer and cause them to quit. You must set out with the mental attitude that you will make it.

In the 1970's there was a popular sitcom called "Laverne and Shirley." This hilarious duo would come into homes all across America making people laugh. One trademark for this show was a little song that they would sing to lift each other's spirits. The song said, "just what makes that little ant think, he can climb a rubber tree plant, anyone knows an ant, can't, climb a rubber tree plant, but he's got High Hopes…"

Decide right now that you will be someone who never gives up. You're going to dream, make plans, follow through and most importantly you will never ever, ever, ever give up!!

What is higher ground?

2

OVERCOMING THE OBSTACLES THAT KEEP YOU FROM CLIMBING

Let me take you back for a moment to the backpacking trip I told you about in Chapter 1. It was my one and only experience backpacking, and although I am not a camping type of person, I must admit I did enjoy it. The beauty of the mountains, the serenity of the peaceful surroundings, and the enormous trees that towered over us all, was quite a sight to see. However, the thing that I enjoyed the most was the sense of accomplishment once we had reached the top of the mountain.

As I think back to that week, I remember many times not wanting to climb the mountain. I remember at the original orientation thinking to myself, "Will this really be worth it, all this work?" I thought of backing out before we even began the trip. Then once we started the trip, there were several times when I thought, "How I would love to stop climbing and turn around and head back down the mountain." Many of us were tired of climbing and our bodies began to ache. The quality of the food was poor, there were no restroom facilities, no showers, it was hot, and did we stink! There were the bugs and snakes that we encountered, and one night we were awoken by a bear, who came into our camp. When that happened, I immediately thought to myself, "This would not happen at the Marriott!"

But as I stated earlier, I am glad we continued the climb; that we did not allow certain circumstances to keep us from going to Higher Ground. Although we felt like giving up, we pressed on and reaped the benefits of all our work. I learned a valuable lesson during that week, that on the road to the top, there will always be opposition.

Whatever your dream or goal is, whatever the road you want to climb, you can be assured there will be opposition. I heard an inspiring story of a 10-year-old girl named Sarah. Sarah was born with a muscle missing in her foot. This unfortunate tragedy caused her to continually be in a brace. She arrived home one day from her elementary school and told her Dad that she had competed in "field day," a day designed with a variety of competitive events for the kids.

Because of her leg support, the father's mind raced as he tried to think of some encouraging words to give to his daughter. Thinking, because of her brace, she probably did not do so well in the competitions. But before he could get out a word, the daughter said, "Daddy, I won two of the races!" The dad couldn't believe it. The daughter went on to say, "But daddy, I had an advantage." The father thought to himself that the teachers must have given her a head start because of her brace. Before he could say anything, the little girl blurted out, "My advantage was that I had to try harder."

That little 10-year-old girl figured out something that thousands of people are still struggling with daily. She knew that she had obstacles and circumstances that made her situation different. But instead of quitting or making excuses for herself, she simply tried harder. Each one of us has our own set of circumstances, obstacles, and oppositions. They stand there like a schoolyard bully taunting our dreams and keeping us from moving forward. Over the years I have seen that the most common obstacles for climbing to Higher Ground are:

❶ FEAR

Fear comes in all shapes and sizes. Fear of the unknown, fear of taking a risk, fear of people, and fear of confrontation. There is the fear of failure, of being embarrassed, of making a mistake, and of letting people down. Fear that you are not good enough, don't measure up, and lack the skills and abilities necessary for the task. Fear of being abandoned, and rejected or hurt by those closest to you. Fear of approaching people, speaking publicly, or sharing your thoughts and ideas in fear of what others may think of you.

I remember my first public speaking experience. I was

14 years old and I was asked to share at a convalescent home. I had prepared all week to share with these people a brief message. I say brief because it was scheduled to last 20 minutes, but I was so scared it only took about six minutes and I was done. I remember stepping up to the microphone and boy was I shaking. In the small crowd was an

FEAR COMES IN ALL SHAPES AND SIZES.

elderly man wearing a red cap. Throughout my entire presentation this man kept yelling out, "Hey sonny, are you from St. Louis?" I had never met the man before, but there he was yelling at me in the middle of my most fearful moment, "Are you from St. Louis?" After that I never thought I would make a life of standing up and sharing to audiences of all ages.

Fear is real. Everyone experiences it at some point in their life. Often the response of people regarding our fear is, "Get over it, just do it, there's nothing to be afraid of, don't worry." These remedies may come in the spirit of love, but let's be honest, they don't really solve the problem. In a moment I will give you some antidotes to help you with fear, but let's look at the second most common obstacle.

❷ INSECURITY

Insecurity varies from fear in that fear is "what" you feel about certain things and insecurity is "why" you feel that way. For instance, I may have a fear of failure but the reason I feel that way is that I am insecure about my abilities.

Insecurity robs us of our potential and ties our feet from marching up the mountain of success.

Insecurities are something that is built into our life over time. The source of our insecurity may come from our upbringing. Growing up with a mom or dad who we could never seem to please or growing up in a home where encouragement and love was rarely ever shared or expressed. Maybe even abuse or abandonment participated in the development of our insecurities. It could have been an experience that took place on a playground many years ago, or maybe a coach that verbalized his or her dissatisfaction with you. Possibly it was a friend who hurt you, a loved one who rejected you, or a spouse who walked away and never came back.

All of these experiences create this enemy of insecurity in our life that prohibits us from developing into the person we would like to be.

❸ CIRCUMSTANCES

Years ago I had the opportunity to share the stage with motivational speaker Rudy Ruettiger. Rudy is best known for his hit movie "Rudy" a story about his life. Rudy is an inspiration to millions. As a young man, he had a desire to play football for Notre Dame. However, his circumstances were piled high against him. He didn't have the test scores or the grades to attend. He was shorter than anyone else on the team, and by his own admittance, the least skilled football player. He fought his way through his circumstances one by one.

Regarding his test scores and grades, he went to a neighboring college and worked hard to get his scores up until finally he was accepted to Notre Dame. In regard to his lack of natural skills and his size, he had to work harder then anyone else. He was a walk-on that served as an extra on the team to help strengthen the scholarship players. He was told he would never get to dress for the game, however, his heart and passion drove his teammates to stand on his behalf, and the coaching staff not only allowed him to dress for the final home game, but to actually play in the game. His name goes down in history as a player for the Notre Dame football team, and his story goes down in history as one of the most inspirational stories of our generation.

> THE ONLY THING YOU CAN CHANGE ABOUT CIRCUMSTANCES IS HOW YOU APPROACH THEM.

You see, it is rare to find someone who is both successful and who complains about their circumstances. But it is common to find those individuals who continually blame their circumstances for their lack of success. Although our circumstances may be rough, they are what they are. If you were born into poverty, there is nothing that will change that now. If you were the oldest and had to work to support the family, there is nothing that will change that now. If you are black, white, woman or man, abused, or taken advantage of, without sounding unconcerned, there is nothing that will change these facts.

Circumstances are what they are. The only thing you can change about circumstances is how you approach them. You can continue to complain, whine, and gripe, but that will not change your circumstances. It will only prevent you from overcoming them. The choice is simple, if you want to go for Higher Ground in your life, you must stop fixing the blame and start fixing the problem.

When it comes to fear, insecurity or circumstances, they are all real and they all serve as obstacles that keep you from climbing your mountain. They are dream stealers, and they will continue to rob you from your journey to the top. Let me give you some antidotes that will help you say goodbye to fear, insecurity and circumstances:

ANTIDOTES TO YOUR FEARS, INSECURITIES, AND CIRCUMSTANCES:

1. Exchange the lies for the truth

The human brain is one of the most fascinating creations from God and it serves your life like a bank. Every day of your life, experiences happen to you and these experiences are deposited into your "mind bank." These deposits that are made become what we call our "memory." When something happens to us, we process that event through our memory, and what has already been deposited in our memories will strongly determine how we respond. For instance, if we have been hurt by someone before and we re-enter a new relationship, we will tend to respond to the new person according to the former experience. From this "mind bank" experience we gain our fears and insecurities in our life.

The answer is obvious. If you have some bad information in your "mind bank," you have to begin exchanging that false information for the truth. Recently my personal computer developed a virus. This virus would negatively affect every disk I inserted, no matter how clean it was. The answer wasn't to get a new computer. I simply had to replace the bad information with good information.

> CONFIDENCE... IT IS A "MUST HAVE" IN YOUR BACKPACK AS YOU JOURNEY UP THE PATH TO HIGHER GROUND.

As I said earlier, our insecurities and fears may come from our upbringing, our experience as a child or youth, a former relationship or many other possibilities. We may have been told that we were no good or we would not amount to anything. We may have been lead to feel that we were not valuable, useful, loveable or acceptable. The only way to deal with these insecurities and fears is do the following:

a. Realize that it is a lie – Anything that tells you that you are not valuable, loveable or acceptable is a lie. It may have been information given to you by someone you know and maybe even love, but it is still a lie.

b. Deposit only positive thoughts – Begin to think differently. Allow your thoughts to dwell on more positive and encouraging things. Try this, when you go to bed, fall asleep thinking wonderful thoughts. Think of and be thankful for your spouse, kids, job, home, health, parents, friends, faith or any other good thing that makes you feel alive!

c. Withdraw only positive thoughts - Now that is easier said than done! There are experiences in our lives that continue to haunt us. These thoughts become a prison of mental horror. We replay them in our mind over and over again. Instead of reliving the hurtful past, begin to withdraw positive thoughts. When you are daydreaming, driving in the car or whenever you do most of your thinking, start withdrawing positive thoughts about yourself and about your circumstances. When the negative thoughts begin to show their ugly heads, say in your mind, "Not today, you'll have to come back another time!"

2. Build confidence in yourself

Confidence is the ultimate remedy for overcoming fear, insecurity, and circumstances. It is a "must have" in your backpack as you journey up the path to Higher Ground. Confidence gives you strength when you are tired, courage when faced with opposition, and a second wind when you feel like giving up. It is difficult to find someone who is succeeding in life, fulfilling wonderful dreams, who is truly climbing the mountain, but lacks confidence. Confidence and success are deeply intertwined and are difficult to separate.

I have two children, Grace, age seven and Aidan, age six. Aidan is young, but already loves to play sports. He is currently involved in Little League baseball and is enjoying every minute of it. One of our favorite activities as a family is to go to his baseball games and watch him play. A few weekends ago, he had his best game. He was catching and throwing very well and he hit three home runs. Now at that age, it isn't too difficult. Because it doesn't matter how far the ball goes, it just matters if it's fair or foul. If it's fair…it's going to be a home run. That's how it goes when you are six years old.

Nevertheless, he had a great game. Since that day, I have noticed that every time he steps out on the baseball field, he is more confident than he has ever been. Every time he goes up to bat now, he's expecting to hit a home run. Every time the ball is hit to him, he's expecting to catch it. His newfound confidence is causing him to practice at home more than ever. The more confident he gets, the better he gets. Confidence is like a momentum machine. Once it's rolling, it is very difficult to stop. The more you have, the stronger the machine becomes.

Obviously, I am not speaking of being arrogant or overly confident, I am simply speaking of having a healthy confidence in yourself and in your abilities and gifts. A newfound, healthy confidence will do wonders for you as you pursue your personal dreams and goals.

Let me give you some practical ideas that will help build confidence in you. These ideas are based on psychological studies that show when a person changes their "physical actions," their "attitude" actually can begin to change, leaving them with renewed confidence. Let me share with you a few ideas:

- **SMILE MORE** – Smiling is excellent medicine for confidence deficiency. If you are lacking confidence, try smiling more. It is very difficult to feel defeated and to have a big smile at the same time. The physical action of smiling will change your attitude! A real and genuine smile will melt away opposition, will give you confidence, and will brighten up the world of those around you. I was recently in a fast food restaurant where the girl behind the counter looked to be having a difficult day. I was next in line, so I said with a big smile, "Hi, how are you today?" She looked at me as if I were the only one who had smiled at her in weeks. She slowly smiled back and said, "I'm fine." I said to her, "Doesn't it feel good to smile?" She sort of laughed and in those few minutes I was at the counter, her entire countenance had changed. Why? Because the physical action of a smile changed her perspective and approach to life.

- **SPEAK UP** – Nothing shows a person's lack of confidence more than when they approach you timidly and say with their head looking down, "Hi, how are you?" It sends a signal that this person really doesn't believe in himself or believe in what he is saying. Practice approaching people with confidence, give them a firm handshake, a big smile, and say a little louder than you normally speak, "How are you?" If they ask you, "How are you doing?" try what author/speaker Zig Ziglar does and says, "I'm outstanding, but improving."

- **MAKE EYE CONTACT** – When you fail to make eye contact when communicating with people, you are sending them a signal. You are saying, "I'm afraid to talk to you, I'm not very confident in myself, I feel inferior next to you." The opposite of that is true as well. When you make eye contact, you are saying, "I believe in myself, I believe in what I'm telling you, I'm above board, and I am confident in myself." Making eye contact not only gives you confidence, it wins you confidence too.

- **EMBRACE LIFE** – Everyday wake up and wrap your arms around life. Embrace the possibilities before you and develop the mindset of a great day. If you think about it, you are already having a great day because you're reading this book, which means you are alive. If you are alive, that means you have countless opportunities. You have the opportunity to love, to give, and to make someone else's day a great one. You can encourage someone today that really needs it, you can start working on your dreams, and start making plans for the future. There are so many opportunities staring you right in the face! So embrace them, embrace life! Yesterday ended this morning, which means today is a brand new day. It is a blank canvas and you are the artist, so begin now - begin to paint your dreams in colors that were made only for you.

These are just a few things you can do to start rebuilding your confidence level - to start feeling better about yourself and your future. Rebuilding your confidence is a great thing because you can start on it immediately. You don't have to wait for anyone or anything!

As you make your decision to search for Higher Ground, you will run into a variety of obstacles ranging from fear to insecurity to overwhelming circumstances. However, if you will choose to exchange the lies for the truth and begin to build up your confidence, it will not matter what you face as you climb the mountain to your dreams. Your momentum will be so strong that any obstacle will seem like a small bump in your personal path of success.

3

BUILDING A GROUP OF CLIMBING COMPANIONS

I told you earlier that one of the dreams that my wife and I had was to plant a successful church. It was in the early part of 1998 that we decided to go forward with that dream. We began to work on all the plans necessary to make this happen. Finances, goals, mission statements, core values, and many other things that are necessary as you take on such a large project. My wife and I realized that in order to climb a mountain this high, we were going to need help. We needed people that would build with us, believe with us, work with us, and become our climbing companions.

During the process of preparation we met with several people sharing our dream and goals for the future. Countless dinners, phone conversations, personal meetings, miles of driving, and sharing with anyone who would listen to the dream. It was an exciting time as we journeyed through the unknown, but probably the most exciting thing to me was sharing with individuals who eventually came on board with us and became a partner in the dream. I knew going into this project that people would be our most precious resource, but I believe I came to appreciate it more than ever.

We built a group of about 50 people who became our partners in this project. Over the next few months we continued to share the vision with them. Sharing about what it meant to be a team, to work together, and to partner with one another. Beyond building a team of people that would assist in accomplishing a goal, these wonderful people became our closest friends. We learned together, laughed together, did social things together, rejoiced with each other, and wept with each other. These people had become, and are still my closest friends. There isn't anything I would not do for any one of them!

We all realized during that time that if you set out to invest in others, they will in turn invest in you. If you sow into someone else's life, they will in turn sow into yours. That is the beauty and importance of having quality people in your life. You are better because you know them, and they are better because they know you. You help each other excel, and soar to places you could never get to on your own.

NEVER UNDERESTIMATE THE NEED OF PEOPLE IN YOUR LIFE.

Whatever your Higher Ground may be, starting a business, advancing a career, financial freedom or whatever your dream is, your greatest asset and richest experience will always be people. Never underestimate the need of people in your life. I have a friend who runs a very large organization and has multiple people under his supervision. Recently, while talking with him he told me that he has made a habit of investing in people's lives. Over the past 25 years he has written on the average of 40 handwritten letters per day. Letters to friends, colleagues, employees, executives, customers, family, and anyone else who came to his mind. I began to think about all of the people he has invested in. People that he has encouraged when they were down, said thank you for a job well done, and said congratulations when they had accomplished a task. He has undoubtedly built a large network of people that believe in him, because he first believed in them.

With all of the investing he has done in people's lives, I wonder if when a need arises in his life, how long it will take for people to rally to his side. If he needed financial assistance, wanted to build a team, needed advice, wanted to open a door that seemed to be shut, or was in need of a favor, he could very easily have hundreds of people by his side ready to help when he called out. Why is this possible? Because he has invested in people's lives.

My friend has not made the tragic mistake that many make. First, he has not burned any bridges. In other words, his life has been spent living with integrity and investing in people's lives. Often people burn bridges with others and soon they find themselves without a bridge to cross. (We will talk more about how to build bridges a little later in this chapter.) Second, he has not looked at one person and said, "I don't need you, or you don't matter." He has realized that every person is loaded with potential. When you negatively or positively affect people, you not only are affecting them, you will ultimately affect who they influence. Let me give you an example of what I mean.

Recently my wife and I purchased a vehicle from a local dealer in the town where we live. We had been looking for some time and one Saturday morning we came across a vehicle that would be suitable for our family. After much discussion we felt that this vehicle was a good purchase. In less than one month that vehicle was back at the dealership with problems. It stayed at the dealership for nearly two weeks. Because it was under warranty we received a loaner car. We were scheduled to spend a few days in the mountains for a special Valentines get away. During that trip we were pulled over by the police because the loaner car had expired tags. Fortunately, the officer let us go and we were not held responsible. Secondly, while we were in the mountains, it began to rain, snow, and we discovered that the loaner car's windshield wipers did not work. Boy, were we upset!

> TAKE CARE OF PEOPLE AND THEY WILL TAKE CARE OF YOU.

After that trip our car was ready, and in less than two

months we were back at the dealership again for more problems with our vehicle. After three weeks in the shop, I was a little frustrated and decided I wanted to speak to the manager about obtaining a different vehicle. Over the course of my conversation I was told that my vehicle was not their responsibility and that they could put me into another vehicle if I gave them additional money. I had never been so rudely treated and felt such a lack of customer care in my life. It goes without saying that we will never buy a vehicle from that dealership again.

In my opinion, the mistake on their side was looking at me as one customer. When I teach at various seminars, I always share with people that every customer has the potential of several more. These people at the dealership must have not realized that I Pastor a rapidly growing church in the city. I have spoken at every major club function and have spoken to most of the public schools in Southern California. So in reality, I am not one customer. I am one customer, who like everyone, has people that they influence. It goes without saying that when someone asks my opinion of this dealership, I will strongly encourage them to look elsewhere.

That is the power of connecting with people in the right way. Take care of people and they will take care of you. Your greatest asset and richest reward will always be your relationships with people. On your road to Higher Ground it's not stepping on people that will get you there quicker, it's building them up, connecting with their hearts, and genuinely caring that will ultimately help you soar to success. In the top selling book, "See You at the Top" author Zig Ziglar says, "You'll always have everything you want in life if you'll help enough other people get what they want." How do we connect with people? How do we help them succeed, which in return will always reap a level of success for our lives? How do we build a high level of positive influence in other people? Here are a few suggestions that will help you C.O.N.N.E.C.T. with others:

CARE WITH A GENUINE SPIRIT

The first step in any successful relationship is genuinely caring about the other person. Not caring about what they can do for you, or where they can take you...but genuinely caring. Not about how much they can help you, or who they are connected with...but genuinely and truly caring. Caring about the person is more than just a card or a nice phone call, it is truly caring about the person and all they are, all they want to become, their struggles, strengths, hurts, concerns, and everything that makes that person who they are.

This first step in connecting with people is checking your own motives. The intent of your heart must be revealed at this stage. Is the motive for this relationship pure? Is it one-sided? Are you merely "appearing" to care based on what they can do for you or do you have a genuine spirit that really cares about the individual? This is where you must do some soul searching and figure out the tough question of why? Why do I want to be near this person?

One of the greatest coaches of all times, Green Bay Packers former head coach Vince Lombardi probably had the pulse on the importance of genuine care more than any other coach who ever lived. Coach Lombardi was quoted as saying, "There are a lot of coaches with good ball clubs who know the fundamentals and have plenty of discipline, but still don't win the game. Then you come to the third ingredient. If you're going to play together as a team, you've got to care for one another. You've got to love each other. Each player has to be thinking about the next guy." Let love be your motive and genuine caring be your action. It is the first step to a successful and fulfilling relationship.

OTHER'S MINDED

Being Other's Minded goes against the grain of our society. We are not conditioned to think of others and, most importantly, to put others first. We are born with a selfish desire to think primarily of our own personal gain. To illustrate this, all you have to do is watch a few toddlers play. When one doesn't get his way, he cries when the toys are out there, it's everyone for themselves. We are all born with this natural instinct of being self-centered.

The best way to combat this natural selfishness and to become Other's Minded is to gain an understanding of the other person's perspective. What are their fears and concerns and how can I better relate to them? I recently left on a small trip and when I was saying goodbye to my family, I picked up my son, who is now six years old, and he said to me, "It sure is high up here." I

THE #1 COMPLAINT AMONG EMPLOYEES ACROSS AMERICA IS THAT THEY DON'T FEEL APPRECIATED.

laughed at his little comment as proud parents often do, but then I got to thinking. He was seeing it from my perspective, which was different from his own.

I began to think about the times I have walked with him in the mall and said, "Hurry up son, your walking too slow." Or the times we took family walks around the block and he would stop and look at the flowers, grass, sprinklers, ants or anything else that intrigued him. Or the time my little girl came running to the front door in fear of a little dog that was about the size of her foot. I never once truly considered my children's perspectives. My son's legs being smaller and his steps being shorter caused him to walk slower. My daughter's fear of a little dog that chased her in the neighborhood. This was their perspective, not mine. It was their fear, not mine. But my job as a parent is to see things from their perspective. This is the only way I can truly connect with them. Other people may have fears and concerns that you do not have. Try to look at it from their perspectives and it will help you connect with them at a higher level.

NURTURE OTHERS

Nurturing people is the third ingredient in connecting with people for successful relationships. Nurturing them does not mean that they are below you, it simply means that you want to help them grow. Think of it as a garden. A garden is a place where seeds are planted. It must have the best of care and be handled with gentleness and kindness. It's partner, the gardener, must be committed to bringing out all the beauty and color that lies deep within the essence of every seed.

Nurturing a garden is a lot like nurturing a successful relationship. It is expressing love, gentleness, and kindness in such a way that it brings out the best in the other person. Let me give you a few examples of ways to nurture your relationships:

- **VERBALIZE ENCOURAGEMENT** – Learn to be someone that encourages people often. Find reasons to encourage and build up those around you. When you see a job well done, when someone goes the extra mile, let them know that you recognized it and verbally express your appreciation and encouragement. Be free and generous with your praise. You will find that people will connect with you quickly and easily when they hear your genuine voice of praise.

- **SEND NOTES OF PRAISE** – Make it a habit to write

out at least 2-3 encouraging notes per day to the people in your life. There is something special about receiving a handwritten note from someone in the mail. It doesn't have to be a long note, just a few sentences telling them how much you appreciate them, or recognize them for something they've done. The #1 complaint among employees across America is that they don't feel appreciated. Do something about that, make the effort every day to value those around you.

* **APPLAUD PUBLICLY** – If you're a leader of any sort, take the opportunity to recognize people publicly. Whatever meetings you host, find time in the agenda to stop and recognize someone for their efforts or success with a certain task. If someone put your meeting room together, or put together the packet or presentation, if there was something good that happened recently, take a moment to honor that person or persons. It will encourage them and inspire them to continue pursuing excellence in their life.

NEVER BREAK TRUST

Trust is something that takes years to gain and moments to lose. Without trust there is no foundation for a successful relationship. Trust is the glue that holds all relationships together. To connect with people, they must trust you. They must believe your words, respect your actions and trust your heart. This kind of trust can only be gained through a life lived with integrity. People often make the fatal mistake of minimizing the importance of integrity by showering their relationships with a charming per-sonality. But what

BE SOMEONE WHO HELPS OTHERS WIN AND IN THE END YOU WILL WIN TOO!

they don't realize is that your personality may win you friends, but without trust, your friends will never climb with you.

Bill Kynes expressed the difficulties of trust when he wrote,

> *We thought we could trust the military,*
> *but then came Vietnam;*
> *We thought we could trust politicians,*
> *but then came Watergate;*
> *We thought we could trust the engineers;*
> *but then came the Challenger disaster;*
> *We thought we could trust our broker,*
> *but then came Black Monday;*
> *We thought we could trust the preachers,*
> *but then came PTL and Jimmy Swaggart.*
> *So who can I trust?*

In our society trust is hard to gain. So live a life that can be trusted. When people can trust you, they will connect with you, climb with you, and ultimately help you reach Higher Ground!

EMPHASIZE THEIR STRENGTHS

Another ingredient in connecting with people is to emphasize their strengths. Help them to see their gifts, abilities, and strong points.

Dr. Robert H. Schuller once wrote, "The truth is that the average 'bottom of the ladder' person is potentially as creative as the top executive who sits in the big office. The problem is that the person on the bottom of the ladder doesn't trust his own brilliance and doesn't, therefore, believe in his own ideas."

Everyone has potential to do great and wonderful things. They are unique creatures of God that are made to do wonderful works. The job of someone who 'connects' with others is to help them understand and believe in their abilities. To help them realize they are a well of fresh water that is waiting to be tapped.

Nathaniel Hawthorne was heartbroken when he went home to tell his wife that he had been fired from his job and that he felt like a failure. His wife responded to this new information by saying, "Good, now you can write your book." He replied with unstable confidence, "Yes, and what shall we live on while I write this book?" To his amazement, she opened up a drawer full of money. He exclaimed, "Where on earth did you get that?" She answered, "I have always known that you are a genius. I knew that someday you would write a masterpiece. So every week out of the money you have given me for house-keeping, I have saved something; here is enough to last us for one whole year." From her confidence in her husband's ability came one of the greatest novels of American litera-ture – The Scarlet Letter.

CREATE AVENUES OF SUCCESS

When you think of the familiar saying, "What goes around, comes around," you tend to think of negative actions. If you are dishonest, lie or cheat, in the end it will come back to haunt you. But have you ever thought of using this familiar saying with a positive action. For instance, if I sow seeds of success in other people's lives, then according to this adage I will reap success for my own. This is true! If you will help those you are connected with succeed in their lives, you will never lack success in your own.

It is a great passion of mine to see others succeed. Whether it be the church where I Pastor or in my personal business, I want to see others succeed. The more I tend to follow this belief of investing in others, the more successful my personal dreams become. It is a personal mission of mine to create avenues of success for the people I work with. I want to help create a path that will successfully lead them to their personal Higher Ground. Listed are two ways to help create avenues of success:

- **PUT WINS UNDER THEIR BELT** – I have a painting in my office that says, "Nothing succeeds like success." This painting rings true that the best momentum in life is a win! Have you ever watched a professional basketball game, when the other team is consecutively scoring and they're on a roll, the opposing team will call time out. Not to just re-group, but to stop the momentum of the other team. Each team realizes the momentum created when the other team is succeeding. A person who truly connects with others helps them to win. They help by setting them up for success. Be someone who helps others win and in the end you will win too!

- **GIVE AWAY THE CREDIT** – Whenever possible, give the credit away. Let it be the other person's idea, the other person's concept, even when you know it was mostly yours. By letting the other person shine, you will give them a confidence they have never felt. Giving away the credit is difficult, especially for those who struggle with insecurity or jealousy. These two emotions will cause you to take the credit rather than give it away. I once read that the mark of a true leader can be noted as follows: "When things go right, they look out the window; when things go wrong, they look in the mirror."

If you struggle with this, try to keep in mind what I mentioned earlier, "What goes around comes around." Let others shine and your personal road to Higher Ground will be lit with success.

TAKE OTHERS WITH YOU ON THE JOURNEY

As you take your personal journey down the road that leads you to all of your dreams and goals, your journey will always be more rewarding and enjoyable if you take people with you. Obviously, you cannot take everyone and, quite honestly, many are not willing to go. They are not willing to pay the price or to sacrifice what is necessary. But for those who are willing to climb with you and become part of your journey, embrace them and take them along for the ride. Let them partner with you and share in the success. You will never accomplish alone all that can be accomplished together. So find the eagles that are willing to fly with you and let them fly. Free of selfishness, jealousy, criticism, and insecurities, take your team of eagles with you and fly on the wings of encouragement, compassion, generosity, and love.

The famous basketball coach Pat Riley once said, "We did not come here to 'compete' with one another, but to 'complete' one another." If you can, grab hold of the concept that people are your most precious resource and begin to treat them that way. If you can, realize that by helping others succeed you succeed as well. If you can, get a handle on what it takes to really connect with people. If you can, see the value of taking others with you on your journey, then you are ready to fly. You can begin to experience all that you once thought was impossible. You are ready to spread your wings and begin the spectacular search for Higher Ground.

4

YOUR ATTITUDE WILL ALWAYS DETERMINE YOUR ALTITUDE

Imagine, if you will, that you are at home, comfortably sleeping in bed. It is 2:30 a.m., and your house is filled with a sense of peace and serenity. Suddenly, you are awaken by the loud ringing of your telephone. You quickly jump out of bed to answer the phone. As you pick the receiver up and place it to your ear, what do you think the information you are about to receive will be...positive or negative?

Your car is making a funny noise so you reluctantly take it to your local mechanic. He takes a quick look at the car and lets you know that further diagnosis will be necessary. You leave the car at the shop and go about your day. A few hours go by and you receive a call from the mechanic. As he begins to tell you what he has found wrong with the car, what is your mind-thinking...positive or negative?

Your boss tells you that he or she would like to see you in their office first thing tomorrow morning. You say yes, as if you have an option, and you head home for the evening. Your boss rarely talks to you and so your mind begins to wrestle with what the subject will center around. You quickly evaluate your progress at work. Your mind gives you an account of your last few days and you begin to re-evaluate over and over, things that were said, projects that were due or anything else that would help you to understand why your boss wants to see you. After a long night of tossing and turning, you get up, get ready, and head for work. When you arrive, you go straight to your boss's office and sit as confident as possible in front of his or her desk. Now tell me, what is going through your mind...positive or negative?

> A POSITIVE ATTITUDE BECOMES THE FUEL TO IGNITE YOUR SPIRIT AS YOU SET YOUR COURSE FOR SUCCESS.

In each of these scenarios there is a good chance that you were quicker to think in the negative rather than to think in the positive. Unfortunately, we as people have a tendency to lean toward a negative mental outlook. A variety of reasons cause us to believe the best for the next guy, but not for ourselves. It's like Murphy's Law. " If it can go wrong, it will." Most people think that for themselves! They feel that opportunities and good fortune happen to others, but are not reserved for them. Have you ever been in a grocery store and looked at two checkout lines and had to make a decision which one you would go to? Then you catch yourself thinking, "It doesn't matter which one I choose, the line

I go in will be slower." We take this kind of negative, pessimistic approach and we try to carry it with us on the road to Higher Ground, but it doesn't work. Negative thinking will prohibit you from reaching your fullest potential, and will weigh you down until you don't want to climb anymore.

The good news is that if a negative attitude is "death" to a person who wants to climb to the top, then a positive and healthy attitude can be "life" to that same person. A positive attitude becomes the fuel to ignite your spirit as you set your course for success. It becomes a compass that guides you on your journey and leads you to higher places. Nothing can exchange the power and potential that is found when one person goes deep inside their soul and discovers the amazing strength that is found in belief.

- The belief in themselves and in their personal potential.

- The belief that anything is possible.

- The belief that if they set their mind to it, they can accomplish something extraordinary.

- The belief that greatness, success, and achievement are not reserved for the few, but are possible for anyone.

  That the Creator has not selected only a handful of people to be achievers, but that in God's infinite wisdom, He placed in the spirit of man the ability to win and to win big!

If attitude is such a powerful tool, then how do we get it?

What steps can we take to exchange a negative attitude for a positive, healthy attitude? Before we begin looking at how to change our attitude, it is important for us to stop and look at where our attitude originates. To discover what the elements in our lives are that have given us our current mental attitude, let me give you the basic foundation for which our attitudes are built:

UPBRINGING

Children specialists will agree that your childhood is strongly related to your overall attitude in life. How you were raised, methods of discipline, morals that were taught, and ethics that were modeled all play a part in developing who you became. When it comes to the development of our attitude, positive or negative surroundings as a child strongly dictate your future mental attitude. Was the overall atmosphere in your home positive or negative? The words that were spoken around the living room or the kitchen table, were they positive or negative? Was your home a place of encouragement or discouragement? Was it a place of image making or image breaking? Was it filled with joy, expectation of good things, and a positive outlook, or was it filled with a doomsday mentality, that nothing ever goes right, and the best way to solve problems is to complain about them?

Chances are, if you were raised in a home where you believed the best about each other, where the outlook on life was positive and healthy, and that instead of complaining about a problem, you figured out a positive solution, then you are most likely a positive person. However, if you were raised in a home where you didn't encourage each other, where the perception of life was relatively negative and where you found complaining and griping as a part of daily conversation, then a negative attitude would be more likely.

In my early twenties I took up the wonderful, yet sometimes frustrating, game of golf. I never took a lesson, I just sort of picked it up and played with different friends. I wasn't very good at the game, but I enjoyed playing. After a while, though, I really wanted to improve my game. I noticed that I had a problem slicing the ball off the tee. Sometimes I would play well, but most of the time it was a disaster. I decided it was time to take lessons. I signed up at a local driving range and I was expecting that the instructor would be my saving grace.

"SELF IMAGE COMES FROM WHAT YOU THINK THE MOST IMPORTANT PERSON IN YOUR LIFE THINKS ABOUT YOU."

After about four to five lessons, the instructor finally told me, "I don't know what's wrong, I've never had a student that I couldn't improve immediately." In essence he was saying your problem is too big and I can't help you.

Naturally, I felt a little let down, but I still enjoyed the game and continued to play. About ten days passed and he called me at my office and said, "Chris, did you ever break your arm?" I was unsure what this meant but I said to him, "Yes, I broke my left arm severely when I was about five years old." He asked me to meet him at the driving range that night, so I did. He told me he was reading a book on golf and there was a story about a man who had broken his arm as a child and because of the accident, one arm was much weaker than the other. The instructor told me to split my grip. I did, and the positive results were immediate.

You see, my problem was that I had been weakened with a broken arm and I had to change my grip. Many people have been weakened with a childhood that was very negative and now it's time to change the grip. They need to begin doing whatever is necessary to change their outlook, to view life differently, to see things in a more positive and healthy way, and to see themselves as capable and full of potential. My golf game needed an instructor to correct it, maybe you will need an instructor (counselor) to help correct any problem you might have. But do whatever is necessary to gain a stronger and healthier attitude. It will become your source of strength in your quest to reach the top.

OTHER PEOPLE

Another part of the construction of our attitude is other people in our lives. People outside of our parents/guardians have a high level of influence and can drastically alter our attitude. They alter our attitude by how they treat us, what they share with us, how they make us feel, and whether or not we are accepted or rejected by them. If they make us feel positive about ourselves, then our attitude tends to be positive. If they make us feel negative, then our attitude tends to be negative. Human behavior studies indicate that "Self image comes from what you think the most important person in your life thinks about you." Throughout your life different people become very important to you and how you feel they view you is the basis for self-image. So if we have negative experiences from other people in our lives, then our attitude toward life will tend to be negative.

Other people can include:

- a coach,

- a close friend,

- a teacher,

- a boyfriend,

- a girlfriend,

- a high school sweetheart,

- a boss,

- a co-worker or

- a variety of people who at some point have had a place of influence in our lives.

Picture in your mind a floor full of children's building blocks. The child puts one piece on top of the other and builds an imaginary building. People in your life are construction workers to your building. They come along and add a piece to your building and assist in creating who you have become.

A little parable entitled, "The Man Who Sold Hot Dogs" evidently dates back to the 1930s, but it bears repeating today. The little story went something like this.

There was a man who lived by the side of the road and sold hot dogs. He was hard of hearing, so he had no radio. He had trouble with his eyes, so he read no newspapers. But he sold good hot dogs. He stood at the side of the road and cried: "Buy a hot dog, mister?" and people bought. He increased his meat and bun orders. He bought a bigger stove to take care of his trade. Business was doing so well that he found it necessary to have his son, who was home from college, help him out. Then something happened.

His son said, "Father, haven't you been listening to the radio? Haven't you been reading the newspapers? The financial situation in Europe is terrible. The situation here in America is even worse." Whereupon the father thought, "Well, my son's been to college, he reads the papers, he listens to the radio, and he ought to know." So the father cut down his meat and bun orders, took down his signs, and no longer bothered to stand out on the highway to sell his hot dogs. And his hot dog sales fell almost overnight. The father said to the boy, "You're right son, we certainly are in the middle of a great depression."

The point is obvious. The father didn't know there was a great depression, his attitude was exactly the opposite. Business was great, his attitude was positive, and life couldn't have been better. But someone comes along that has a place in his life, says a few words, and now the father's attitude changes. People have a place in building your attitude! It's up to you whether or not you want to add the building block they bring to your life or dismiss it. It's up to you to separate the truth from the lies, what is right and what is wrong. A rule of thumb is; if what people say or do to you doesn't build you up, challenge you to be better, and come in the spirit of love, then maybe it's not worth adding to the construction of your attitude.

SURROUNDINGS

It seems that most people, if they are not careful, can find themselves submitting to the power of pessimism. This really isn't that hard to do when you consider the surroundings most of us face each day in our lives. A few years back I was sitting in a hotel room watching T.V. During the commercial break came an advertisement of the news that was coming up in the next hour. The broadcaster doing the quick commercial said, "Coming up next on the 11:00 p.m. news, three people are dead in a high speed accident, stock prices are threatening a possible recession, and researchers are saying that your drinking water may be connected to cancer." Now with news like that, it isn't too difficult to get trapped in the web of negativity.

From the news we watch, to the gossip we hear, from the constant complaining of those around us, to the traffic we sit in, there is a constant war against positive and healthy attitudes. Pressures, problems, and people continue to chip away at our attitude, leaving our mental perception struggling to stay positive. But the fact remains, if you are going to reach for Higher Ground, you cannot leave the power of attitude at the bottom of the mountain. Your attitude determines if you are on the way out or on the way up. The following short poem describes it best:

> "THINK YOU CAN, THINK YOU CAN'T, EITHER WAY YOU ARE RIGHT."

If you think you are beaten, you are;
If you think you dare not, you don't;
If you like to win, but think you can't,
It is almost certain you won't.
Life battles don't always go
to the faster or stronger man.
But in the end, the one who wins,
is the one who thinks he can.

We now understand how important a positive attitude is on your journey to Higher Ground. But how do we get it? What steps can we take to both improve and grow our positive attitudes? Let me give you a few practical steps that will help you obtain the kind of attitude that will keep you soaring to the top:

❶ ELIMINATE NEGATIVE SELF-TALK

Your first and foremost lesson in gaining a new optimism is eliminating negative self-talk. Author and motivational speaker, Keith D. Harrell, once said, "The loudest voice we hear is our own." There are many voices we hear, but the one inside our mind is the strongest voice in our lives. It helps to chart our course in either optimistic thinking or pessimistic thinking.

We are all guilty at times of hosting a variety of negative self – statements. See if you can identify with any of these...

- **I am too old to do anything else in my life**
- **I am not smart enough to do this**
- **I just know it won't work out**
- **I just don't have the time or energy**
- **I'm not as good or capable as the next person**
- **If it can go wrong, it will**
- **It probably won't happen**
- **I just can't do it**

Is there any statement that you can add to this list?

What is the one thing you find yourself saying over and over again in your mind? Whatever the statement is, if it doesn't encourage you or bring out the best in you, it's time to eliminate it from your mind. Choosing to be more positive than negative reminds me of a story I once heard.

A man walking through the local park stopped to observe a little league baseball game. He looked up at the scoreboard to see how the game was going. He saw that the score was 15-0. He decided to walk over to the dugout of the losing team. They were out in the field, but there were a few of them sitting on the bench. He asked one of the boys, "How are things going?" The little boy with a big smile said, "Great." The man said, "You seem fairly positive even though your team is losing 15-0." The little boy, without missing a beat said, "Of course I'm positive, we haven't been up yet." Now there's a little boy who has the right perspective. He hasn't fallen into the snare of negative talk. He believes the best about himself and those around him. He reminds me of something I read recently that simply said, "Think you can, think you can't, either way you are right." Learn to eliminate the heavy burden of self-talk and it will free you to climb even quicker on your journey to Higher Ground.

❷ MAKE A CONSCIOUS CHOICE TO RISE ABOVE YOUR CIRCUMSTANCES

As I mentioned earlier, Higher Ground for me was starting a church in the city of Corona, California. Though it has been the most exciting adventure I have ever taken, it has not been without a few bumps in the road. There have been a few things that have taken place on my journey to Higher Ground that have weighed me down at times.

I remember it was just a few days before the "Grand Opening" of this church. We had sent out thousands of promotional videos and brochures inviting the community to join us. The outstanding team of people, who I was privileged to work with, were ready. We had done all we could and were expecting and believing for great things. We had signed a lease to use a small facility as our place to hold services. Just about a week before our first public service, I received a phone call from the city inform-

> IF YOU WANT TO SOAR LIKE AN EAGLE, THEN YOU HAVE TO BE CAREFUL NOT TO WALK WITH THE TURKEYS.

ing us that we were not allowed to use our rented facility for church services. I immediately headed down to their offices to discuss the matter. I pleaded my case and literally begged them to reconsider. I told them we had spent thousands of dollars and all the promotional materials included the address of this facility. After much pleading and a little begging, they told me they would reconsider and they would let me know.

As the leader of this adventure, I had to be positive. I had to "choose" and make a conscious decision that my attitude was going to be positive. Was it easy? NO! Did I feel positive? Not really. But I had to make a choice to believe the best and I wasn't about to let this one issue block my path to Higher Ground. My mind reflected back to the words of Michael de Montaigne, "I am an optimist. It does not seem too much use being anything else." By the end of the day I received permission from the city. I later found out that in normal circumstances it could take up to two weeks to receive permission to use the facility, but in our case it took a day. Throughout the short history of this church there have been a few circumstances that could have gotten the best of us. But we chose each time not to let circumstances control our destiny or overpower our thinking. I believe being optimistic can best be described in this way:

"Real optimism is aware of problems, but recognizes the solutions; knows about difficulties, but believes they can be overcome; sees the negatives, but accentuates the positives; is exposed to the worst, but expects the best; has reason to complain, but chooses to smile."

You see, being an optimist is a choice. You make a conscious choice to be positive no matter what circumstances you face. You can be negative...but what good could possibly come out of it? On your personal path to Higher Ground there will always be bumps in the road. Things may not always go right or go your way, but you must choose to stay positive through it all. As I've said before, "You can be happy and stuck in traffic or be mad and stuck in traffic, but either way you are stuck in traffic." So no matter what circumstance you face, always choose the powerful tool of optimism.

❸ ASSOCIATE WITH POSITIVE PEOPLE

You have heard the statement before, "Birds of a feather flock together." If you want to be positive and remain positive, you must choose to associate with positive people. It is nearly impossible to find two people associating with each other where one is highly positive and one is highly negative. Positive people don't want to always hear how bad things are. They want to embrace life in a big way and they choose to see opportunity wherever they look.

Throughout your life you may have been raised in negative surroundings. Your upbringing may have been with individuals who had a knack of finding the worst in every situation. But if you're an adult, now you get to choose who you associate with. It is your choice to allow certain people into your circle of influence. I have hundreds of acquaintances and multiple friends, but I have only a few people that I allow into what I call 'my circle of influence.' The 'circle of influence' is not necessarily who I influence, but who I allow to influence me. These people are positive, they believe the best, they see opportunities not obstacles, they want the best for my life, they add value to me, and they want me to succeed. They are not complainers or whiners. They don't gossip and a critical spirit has not trapped them. In my eyes, these people are eagles, they are "10s" and I love to associate with these people. But keep in mind, it's my choice to allow these people into my 'circle of influence,' just as it is your choice to allow positive thinkers or negative thinkers to be part of your association.

When Henry Ford wanted to get unbreakable glass for his cars, he wouldn't see any of the experts. They knew too many reasons why it couldn't be done. He said, "Bring me the eager young person who doesn't know the reasons why unbreakable glass cannot be made." The result was he got his unbreakable glass. Henry Ford didn't want to associate with those individuals who didn't see a way. He wanted to be around those that believed it was possible.

Think about the people who are closest to you right now. Not your family members, but work associates, social friends, etc. Are these people positive and do they seem to always find the best in every circumstance? If the answer is no...then the first place you need to look at is yourself. Remember that you always attract what you are, not necessarily what you want. If the people around you have a tendency to be more negative than positive or if they fail to bring out the best in you, there is a good chance that you have attracted what you are. That should be a warning sign that you need to start the changing process to a more positive way of life. If you want to be a "10," associate with

"10s." If you want to soar like an eagle, then you have to be careful not to walk with the turkeys. Because the principle of association never fails...you become like those who are closest to you.

My final thought for you on this issue of "Attitude" is something I learned while attending a conference with Zig Ziglar. He said, "Wake up every morning and say out loud, 'today is going to be the best day of my life.'" This may seem a little uncomfortable at first, but after a while you will begin to discover what I have discovered that it works. That waking up each morning and starting off with the right positive, mental attitude will make a big difference in your life. Begin to observe why life is so great, think about the positive things that are in your life right now. The people that you love and how fortunate you are to have them in your life. That you live in a country of freedom and opportunity. That you may have a car to drive, a home to live in, clothes to wear, and food to eat. That although life may not be going perfect, you are better off than the one-third of the world who will go to bed hungry tonight. As you drive home from work, think about the job you have, the pay you earned, and be thankful. Then, when your head hits the pillow in the safety of your home and you were fortunate to live another day in this magnificent world, you will wake up again tomorrow and say out loud, "Today is going to be the best day of my life."

5

STAYING MOTIVATED ON THE MOUNTAIN

As you search for Higher Ground in your life, there will be times when you feel like giving up. Times when you feel like it's pointless and you just don't want to try anymore. You'll feel like it's too hard to keep climbing and you'll simply want to quit. The question is not whether you are going to feel like this at various times in your life, the real question is, "What will be your response to these feelings?" Will you stay motivated enough to climb the mountain and finish the journey or will you find yourself lacking the motivation to continue upward?

I'm reminded of a story my friend told me about a young boy whom the schoolyard bully was picking on everyday. Each day this bully would steal this young boy's lunch money and the little boy was tired of being picked on. One day on his way home from school he noticed a sign advertising free karate lessons. He inquired within and began taking his lessons immediately. After about a week of taking lessons, the instructor informed him that the free lessons was only good for a week and that each lesson would now cost $5 per session. The little boy didn't have the money and he figured it would be harder to come up with the money for the lessons than it would be to pay the schoolyard bully so, he quit.

The moral of the story is obvious. This little boy lacked the motivation and found it easier to take the path of least resistance. Unfortunately, many people do that. They start off with great intentions, but lose their motivation. "I'm going to start a new business, change careers, improve my relationships, establish a stronger faith, develop a non-profit organization, or make a dream become reality." Maybe you've said this or something like this, maybe you have even started taking some steps toward these objectives. But in the case of thousands of people, their good intentions weren't good enough.

Before I share with you about "how" to get motivated and stay motivated, let me share with you some incredible benefits of being a person of motivation...

- **ENERGY** – People who are motivated tend to have a higher level of energy. It's almost as if they don't need as much sleep. It's not that they are running on pure adrenaline, they simply seem to have a higher level of energy than those who lack motivation.

- **RECOGNITION** – People who are motivated stand

out. They are recognized for their motivation and their desire to embrace life and all it has. People admire them, and they find others willing to assist them in reaching their goals.

- **OPTIMISTIC** – Motivated people are optimistic. Their outlook on life tends to be filled with optimism. They see opportunities around them, they encourage those they come in contact with, and they add value to people and to situations. Motivated people are less likely to allow negativity to have a place in their lives.

- **ACHIEVEMENTS** – Highly motivated people usually achieve more. They go after tasks with greater zeal and accomplish more on a day by day basis. They attack their goals and "to do" lists with greater ambition than those lacking motivation.

- **HEALTH** – Those who are motivated are more likely to be healthy because they realize the value of fitness. They have noticed the difference in their level of energy when they make health a priority, so because they are motivated to be better, they are motivated to feel better.

- **STABILITY** – Motivated people are more likely to be stable in their everyday life. This is because they are more focused and know how to stick to the job. They do not waver whenever the ground beneath them begins to shake. They have learned how to stay strong and focused regardless the size of the storm. These are just a few of the incredible benefits reserved for those who choose to make motivation a part of their life.

The reality is, "Motivation" is an absolute must if you desire to reach Higher Ground. However, if you think about it, everyone is motivated by something different. What motivates you may not motivate the next person. Some are motivated by money, that is, the reason they live and work, to obtain more money. Others are motivated by recognition. They have a desire to be recognized and will do what it takes to obtain it. Still others are motivated by service, they have a passion to help people and that is their simple and pure motive.

What I'm simply conveying is that we are all motivated by different things. Our unique human spirits are filled with a variety of passions, strengths, dreams, desires, and motivating factors. What excites your life and makes you tick will not do it for the next person. These motivating factors are what will determine your behavior. Your actions will be a direct result of what motivates your heart.

My wife and I are perfect examples of two people being motivated in different areas. Over the years I have realized the lesson I am now trying to share, that we are all motivated differently. Recently, we were having a discussion of our personal desires for our life. My wife shared that one of the most important events that could happen in her life would be to raise our two children in a loving home with a solid and active faith in God. Among other motivations, her desire for our children is a high priority and she is motivated by this goal. I share this goal with her but I found myself realizing, more than ever, we share different passions and desires. Speaking, writing books, and helping to resource people for success motivate me. But she does not share these same passions. We are unique creatures of God and he has wired us each very different.

FIND YOUR MOTIVATION

Everyone has some type of motivation. They have something that drives them and serves as a passion in their heart. When you think of someone like Walt Disney, you think of someone who had a desire to make children happy and allow adults to feel like kids again. This desire kept him motivated through all the obstacles to keep pressing on when others would have quit. When you think of Bill Gates and his desire to see a P.C. in the home of every person in America, this desire became his motivation and his means for success. When you think of Hewlett Packard as a company that started in a garage by two college kids with the motivation to provide inventions that would make life more convenient, you begin to realize that each motivation is different and unique. You also realize that these pioneers took

YOUR MOTIVES WILL REVEAL YOUR CHARACTER AND YOUR CHARACTER IS THE PREMISE FROM WHICH ALL TRUE SUCCESS IS BUILT.

their motivation and turned it into success.

Find your motivation, find the thing that thrills your heart more then anything else. You will find that it will be easier to stay motivated with something you like rather than something you dislike. You will notice that you do not tend to burn out on your strength, but you burn out on your weaknesses.

CHECK YOUR MOTIVES

The question you always want to ask yourself when it comes to your personal motivations or your personal Higher Ground, is why? Why do I want this thing for my life? What motivation do I have to obtain this certain Higher Ground? You might say, "I want to be rich...ask why? I want to be famous...ask why? I want to have my own business...ask why?" Your motives will reveal your character and your character is the premise from which all true success is built. The last thing you want is to have your personal Higher Ground be made with a foundation of self-ishness, greed or pride.

Joe Griffith writes in his book, "Speakers Library of Business" about the infamous Wall Street arbitrageur, Ivan Boesky. He writes that Mr. Boesky was widely known for making money and advocating his belief in business greed. His greed led him to a criminal act which resulted in time served in jail, fines, and a ban on practicing business. Joe Griffith writes, "Amassing money or goods for your own sake may reward in the short term, but over the long haul it destroys those companies and individuals who give in to it." His motivation was making money, but his "motive" was greed. Lesson…always check your motive for whatever it is you want. Keep it free from greed, pride or selfishness!

Now that you realize the benefits of being a person of motivation and how important it is to find your motivation and to keep your motives in check, let me share with you some practical ideas to keep you motivated on your journey to Higher Ground:

STAYING MOTIVATED

Stay motivated by viewing your climb one step at a time

Let me take you back for a moment to the backpacking trip I discussed earlier. When we arrived at the mountain, I looked up to the top as a beginning climber and said to myself, "There is no way that I can climb that mountain. It's too high, too hard, and I simply cannot climb it." Well, as I told you earlier, we did. We struggled, got tired, felt like quitting at times, but we climbed it. We made it to the top of the mountain, and you know where it all started…at the bottom of the mountain when we decided to take our first step. You will find your mountain will be easier to climb when you do it one step at a time. If you look at the entire mountain, it can be overwhelming at times, but if you look at it in bite size pieces, it's easier to swallow.

In my quest to plant a church there were many things to

be done and quite frankly the entire picture was over-whelming. A team to build, money to raise, facilities to secure, equipment to buy, promotional materials to design, leaders to grow, and all of this was to be done with no money and no people. This was a giant mountain and could have easily overtaken me to the point where I would feel like giving up. The answer for me came in taking this mountain and breaking it down into one step at a time. You see, the ultimate goal was the finish line, but the best way for me to get to the finish line was simply breaking it down step by step. If you can learn to break down your Higher Ground goals into one step at a time, you will find the task of staying motivated a little easier.

STAY MOTIVATED THROUGH PERSONAL GROWTH

Stanford University did a study and concluded that only 5% of people that set out to implement something into their lives ever do it. The reason 95% of people never finish the task is that they simply lack the resources to stay motivated long enough to accomplish their goals. That is why I am a firm believer in consistently feeding yourself for personal growth. Many people have said to me, "Chris you are going to teach another motivational topic, don't you know that after awhile the people will go back to normal?" My response to that is, "Of course I know that people will eventually go back to the way they were, but that is why they need constant motivation. You don't take a shower once and say, "That's it." You make an effort to stay physically clean, as you do to stay highly motivated.

Here's a list of things I recommend to you to stay on a path of personal growth...

- **READ BOOKS** – Find books that motivate you and keep you growing and read them.

- **LISTEN TO TAPES** – Purchase tapes from your favorite speakers and listen to them over and over until they get down into your spirit.

- **ATTEND SEMINARS** – Make it a habit to attend at least 3-4 seminars per year. These events will help to charge you up and keep you going.

- **ASSOCIATE WITH MOTIVATED PEOPLE** – I've mentioned this before, but it bares repeating. You become like those you associate with. If you want to stay motivated, associate with motivated people.

- **SPIRITUAL RENEWAL** – For me personally, one of the greatest forms of motivation comes from my deep faith in God, who is my #1 source for motivation. If God isn't part of your life, you should deeply consider it...He can do far more in your life than you ever imagined.

Make personal growth a lifetime journey. Never stop learning and growing. It will keep you motivated as you conquer each step toward Higher Ground.

STAY MOTIVATED BY MOTIVATING OTHERS

Jaime Escalante was a teacher at Garfield High School in East Los Angeles and he is the man behind the movie "Stand and Deliver." His story is one of inspiration and hope. Garfield High had been known for its violence, graffiti, and gang members. It had been a school filled with underachievers and led by a principle who didn't understand what it took to bring out the best. In the fall of 1978, Escalante searched throughout the 3,500 students of Garfield High to establish the first calculus class. He was able to round up 14 students to take the class and prepare for the AP (Advanced Placement) exam. After much work he had only five students take the AP exam and only two passed.

YOUR LIFE HAS PURPOSE AND THERE ARE DREAMS THAT ONLY YOU CAN LIVE OUT.

In 1980 he did it again and managed to get 15 students for his calculus class, and this time 14 passed. He worked before and after school with these students year after year, believing the best in them and in their ability to succeed. In 1983 he helped 31 students pass the AP exam and in 1987, 129 students took the exam with 85 receiving college credit. This former school of underachievers had now produced 27% of all passing AP exams by Mexican-Americans in the entire United States.

Jaime Escalante is the perfect example of someone climbing for Higher Ground but being faced with difficulty. He had every right to lose his motivation and to give up...many of us would have. But he stayed motivated by realizing the power of motivating others. You see, when you can help others achieve their goals and bring out the best in them, it helps you to achieve your own. You've heard it said that, "You get out of life what you put into it." Put into the lives of others great motivation and you will get out of life great motivation. You want to stay motivated? Be committed to motivate others.

STAY MOTIVATED BY HOW YOU FEEL

There is something to be said for the statement "Dress for Success." But it's not only how you dress, it's how you feel. Your physical body and your appearance make you feel good. When someone comes up to you and says, "Have you been losing weight?" How does that make you feel? It makes you feel great. When someone comes up to you and says, "Is that a new shirt? I really like those shoes your wearing." It has a way of lifting your spirits.

The exact opposite is true, if you feel physically down and you don't feel your appearance is at its best, it has a way of bringing you down. It can actually serve as a de-motivator. It robs you of staying motivated and on top of your game. One of the things I like to do when I have an extra special speaking engagement, is to buy something new.

Maybe a tie, or a new pair of socks or a shirt. I buy something that when I put it on, it makes me feel good. If you want to stay motivated, choose to feel good. Exercise, dress nice, keep your appearance displaying success, and you will find it an easier task to stay motivated on your journey to the top.

Whatever you have to do to stay motivated, do it. Read books, listen to tapes, attend seminars, associate with motivated people, think motivated, speak motivationally, place motivational statements around your home, office or in your car. However you do it is up to you, but stay motivated. Your life has purpose and there are dreams that only you can live out. They have been placed in your heart and you are the one that destiny has called to fulfill this purpose. Don't be a quitter, stay focused and motivated on the task at hand.

I came across this poem called "Don't Quit." I challenge you to rewrite it and place it where you can see it everyday and let it be the anthem to your motivation to never ever stop.

DON'T QUIT

When things go wrong, as they sometimes will,
When the road you're trudging seems all uphill.
When the funds are low and the debts are high,
And you want to smile but you have to sigh.

When care is pressing you down a bit,
Rest if you must, but don't you quit.
Life is strange with its twists and turns,
As everyone of us sometimes learns,
And many a failure turn about,
When he might have won had he stuck it out.
Don't give up though the pace seems slow.
You may succeed with another blow.
Success is failure turned inside out,
The silver tint of the clouds of doubt,
And you never can tell how close you are,
It may be near when it seems so far,
So stick to the fight when you're hardest hit.
It's when things seem worse,
That you must not quit.

6

DEVELOPING THE HABITS THAT WILL TAKE YOU TO THE TOP

In February of 1998, in Nagano, Japan the most highly trained athletes began to arrive for the biggest sporting event in the world...the Olympics. The Olympics is the one time when all of the world becomes united under the spirit of competition. Athletes, who have trained all their lives in hopes to win the Gold, come to compete with people from foreign countries, not speaking the same dialect, but speaking the same language of excellence in their fields of competition.

America was hopeful to win several medals in various events throughout the Winter Olympics. Of all the sporting events and athletes, America's eyes seemed to turn toward two very young and competitive individuals in the competition known as Ladies Figure Skating. The two athletes were Tara Lipinski, age 15, and Michelle Kwan, age 17. These two individuals were highly favored to medal in their event, but the question came down to whom would win the Gold.

As they often do in the Olympics, brief biographies of Tara Lipinski and Michelle Kwan were given throughout the competition. These biographies would show the rigorous schedules that these young ladies had to keep. Waking up at 4:00 a.m. and training for 2-3 hours before school, then after school training for another 3-4 hours, doing their homework and heading for bed, only to wake up in the morning and do it one more time.

Their training included running, skating, eating right, working out and doing it over and over again. Day after day, week after week, month after month, and year after year. Their training never stopped. They realized that in order to win the Gold, there was a price to be paid. If you wanted to stand on the platform and hear your country's anthem ring with the Gold around your neck, you would have to keep up a schedule and routine that others were unwilling to do.

In their biographies, the schedules and routines seemed similar, both worked very hard and sacrificed greatly. There was one thing I noticed while watching the personal interviews. Tara Lipinski said in her interview that she had dreamed of standing on the platform with the Gold. She had thought about it every day for the past several years. It was a passion inside of her that she could not escape. In the interview with Michelle Kwan, I noticed one thing was different. When asked about her expectations regarding a Gold medal, she said that she was just happy to be at the

Olympics, and we will see what happens from here. A big difference from Tara Lipinski who literally dreamed of winning the Gold. They both had outstanding work habits, but there was still the habit of dreaming, believing, and expecting that seemed to separate them. The result was that Tara Lipinski did walk away with the Gold, and Michelle Kwan received the Silver.

Habits are a big part of the level of success an Olympian will experience, and it will play a major role in your personal success as you journey to Higher Ground. The ability to create the right working habits may be the single most important tool you will need. As I have discovered for myself in my personal journey, the right working habits will eventually produce the results I have been seeking. John Mason in his book, "Know your Limits and Ignore Them" writes, "People spend half their time telling you what they are going to do and the other half making excuses why they didn't do it." I couldn't agree with that more! But if I may be so bold to add to John's statement by saying, "One of the reasons people don't complete what they say they are going to do is that they have not developed the necessary habits to get it done." They set out with good intentions to accomplish a certain task or obtain a heart felt dream, but

> "PEOPLE SPEND HALF THEIR TIME TELLING YOU WHAT THEY ARE GOING TO DO AND THE OTHER HALF MAKING EXCUSES WHY THEY DIDN'T DO IT."

they don't develop the habits necessary to see those dreams become reality.

Not setting yourself up with the right habits is as foolish as a fitness expert not developing the habit of eating right. Or a boxer setting out to win the championship, but not developing the work habits that will get him there. Maybe your Higher Ground includes buying a house, early retirement, changing careers, starting a business, learning a second language or a new instrument, becoming a leader or founding an organization. Whatever worthwhile dream you possess, it will require you to develop the right habits. Ignoring this principle will set you up for failure every time.

FACTS ABOUT HABITS...

TRUTH 1 Good Habits are hard to make

Have you ever made a New Year's resolution to begin eating right or exercising daily, only to find yourself right back where you started in under a month? I was speaking to a friend of mine who oversees several fitness centers and I could not believe how many people he told me were members at each fitness center. I asked him, "Why do you sign up so many people? There is no way they could all fit in here if they all came at the same time." He said, "We are counting on the majority of them not following through with their commitment to begin working out." I thought to myself, isn't that amazing, that the success of this fitness center is dependent on the average American's inability to follow through.

Good Habits are a lot like a stamp. They are only good when they stick to something. Good Habits are good, but their value and their worth comes in the ability to stick with it. That is why so many people start off with the right idea, but can't finish the job. Because Good Habits are hard to make. If they were easy, everyone would be doing them. People that are dream builders...people like you, must be willing to take the time and effort to instill into their lives the "Good Habits."

Take a moment to complete the exercise on the following page. On the "Goal" side write down one thing you would like to accomplish (Purchase a home, Start a Business, Get in Shape, etc...). Then on the other side write down the Habits necessary to see this task completed.

For instance, if you were to say that you wanted to purchase a home, you may need to create the Good Habit of budgeting, saving, and cutting back. Or if you want to get in shape, you may need to write down the habits of eating right, exercising daily, etc. Complete this exercise before going any further in this chapter.

Goal: **Necessary Habits to Accomplish the Goal**

1. _____   1. _____

2. _____   2. _____

3. _____   3. _____

This is how it works if you are going to succeed with what you are wanting to achieve. You set out with your goals and then figure out the habits necessary to accomplish those goals. If you are unwilling to develop the Right Habits, chances are your dream will remain a dream until your willing to pay the price. Good Habits are hard to make; but anything worth having takes work!!

TRUTH 2 Bad Habits are hard to break

Not only are Bad Habits hard to break, they also seem a lot easier to make than Good Habits. Simple things, like biting your nails, become a habit that is difficult to break. But there are other habits that become part of our lives that cost us a lot more than biting your nails. These Bad Habits steal from our dreams, time, and finances. Horace Mann once said, "Habit is a cable; we weave a thread of it every day and at last we cannot break it." These Bad Habits include:

• OVERSPENDING,

- OVEREATING,

- WATCHING TOO MUCH T.V.,

- PROCRASTINATING,

- SMOKING,

- DRINKING,

...and the list goes on.

The price to break these habits are high, but not nearly as high as the price we pay to keep them. You always pay a price for staying the same!!

I once read about the settlers who came to live in the Western U.S. Roads in those days were often just wagon trails. These trails often grew very deep after much use by wagons. The trails posed serious problems for those who attempted to journey on them. On one of the windy paths was posted a sign which read: "Avoid this rut or you'll be in it for the next 25 miles!" Isn't that a lot like a Bad Habit. We begin practicing them not realizing the serious problem they will impose. Just like the wagon, we can't go down another path until we get out of the one we are in. Bad Habits are hard to break, but they must be broken for anyone who wants to climb the path to Higher Ground.

> SUCCESSFUL PEOPLE ARE SIMPLY WILLING TO DEVELOP THE HABITS THAT UNSUCCESSFUL PEOPLE ARE UNWILLING TO DEVELOP.

The Right Habits separate

There is nothing that separates successful people from unsuccessful people more than this one word, "Habits." I have found that the difference is that successful people are simply willing to develop the Habits that unsuccessful people are unwilling to develop. One of the greatest, if not the greatest basketball legend of all times, is Michael Jordan. He is an incredible athlete, an outstanding competitor, a leader, and team player. It has been said that Michael Jordan made it a "Habit" that, when everyone else was through practicing, he would stay around and spend an hour or more practicing free throws. It was this habit that assisted him in becoming a legend. That's what the Right Habits do, they separate the good from the great, the ordinary from the extraordinary.

Paine Webber has a slogan that reads, "Invest with discipline." Their idea is that, if you will make it a Habit to invest on a regular basis, over time you will become financially secure. The Right Habits make a difference. If you can create the Habit of reading 15 minutes per day on a self-improvement book or a book on the area you want to grow in, can you imagine how much you would learn after only one year. The Right Habits make a difference. What if you decided to make exercise a Habit, but only did it for 20 minutes per day, would it make a difference? Of course it would! The Right Habits make a difference!

What if you got in the Habit of showing up to work 30 minutes early everyday? You would get more done and make a tremendous impression on your supervisor. The Right Habits make a difference. What if you got into the habit of writing two "encouraging" notes per day to people that you work with, colleagues, friends, future clients, mentors or anyone else in your life? Would it make a difference? Absolutely! The Right Habits make a difference. What if you got in the Habit of making a "to do" list at the end of each day and the following day you actually did it? Would it make a difference? Of course it would! The Right Habits make a difference.

The Right Habits, when regularly practiced, will make a difference in your life. They will set you apart from the pack, they will cause you to excel. The Right Habits will lift you slowly and surely to a new level in your life. Like a flower in the garden, you plant a seed and water it daily. Your habit of nurturing is necessary for the life of that potential flower. After much consistent and daily care, you will eventually reap the rewards of your work and a flower will blossom. The same is true with your dreams. Plant them in your heart, water them with the Right Habits, and eventually they will produce something beautiful in your life. That's the power of habits, and that's the difference they'll make.

You now understand how the Right Habits can connect you to your dreams and how Bad Habits can keep you from your dreams. Now it's time to look at some practical suggestions that can help you in ridding yourself of the Bad Habits and developing the life changing practice of Good Habits.

SEEK AN ACCOUNTABILITY PARTNER

What is accountability? Accountability is being responsible to finish what you said you would do. If you open up a charge account or if you take out a loan, you are "accountable" for that loan or that charge account. Whatever payment is due, you are the one who is responsible. Your accountability partner in this case is the bank.

> SOMETIMES YOU HAVE TO CHOOSE BETWEEN WHAT IS GOOD AND WHAT IS BEST!

They will be the one to hold you accountable to finish what you said you would do. That's accountability and that's what an accountability partner does, they hold you to your word.

If you are going to be committed to creating the "Right Habits" in your life, the ones that are going to lead you to Higher Ground, you will need to find yourself an accountability partner. Someone you trust, who wants the best for your life and who will take the time and effort to keep you accountable for what you said you would do. Accountability partners don't just happen. They don't knock on your door one day and say, "Hey, I would like to hold you accountable." You must seek them out and approach them or you will never have an accountability partner.

A few years ago I did this exact thing, I found someone whom I trust and whom I know wants what's best for my life, and I asked him if he would hold me accountable. I am the one who has to set the meetings, and I am the one who has to be willing to be truthful and to hear the some-times difficult truth about areas of my life that need improving. This person has become a close friend and men-tor, and I am farther along in life because I have sought him out for accountability.

Begin thinking about someone who can become your accountability partner. Make sure it is someone you know will be truthful with you. Share with this individual your dreams, goals, and aspi-rations. Show them your plan and the Habits necessary to obtain your goals and have them keep you accountable to these new Habits. Similar to a nutrition consultant who keeps you accountable and on track with your fitness goal, that's what your accountability partner will do for you. They will help to keep you on track with the daily disciplines necessary for success.

> "TODAY IS THE TOMORROW THAT YOU SAID YESTERDAY YOU WOULD GET IT DONE."

ELIMINATE TIME WASTERS

I recently came across an article in Self Magazine. It was an article on how the littlest change in your dietary habits can make a big difference. Here is what the article said:

"If you just substitute high calorie offenders for similar tasting, lower calorie choices, the weight loss can still be significant. Give up one teaspoon of cream in your coffee and lose 6 pounds a year, or switch to a similar amount of skim milk and lose 5 pounds. Give up a glazed donut a day and lose 25 pounds a year, or switch to a medium sized bran muffin and lose 11 pounds in a year. Skipping a teaspoon of butter on a daily bagel will leave you 11 pounds lighter at year's end, or change to similar amount of cream cheese and drop 5 pounds. Some other items you can drop and save on are a 12 ounce can of soda a day and forget 17 pounds in a year; a 1.2 ounce chocolate bar a day saves you 12 pounds in 18 months."

What's the point of this illustration…even the smallest change in a Bad Habit can make a difference!! It's true with food and it's true with your daily life. There are Habits that could change, schedules that could be adjusted and even the slightest change could make a significant difference in your life. The key to this concept is to narrow down the list of what I call "Time-Wasters." Take a moment to figure out what things in your life waste your time and keep you from doing the habits necessary for success. Keep in mind that Time-Wasters are not always bad, they just might not be what's best for your life. Sometimes you have to choose between what is good and what is best!

Take some time to think this through. What are the Time-Wasters in your life? Could be as simple as T.V. or searching the Internet. Maybe it's activities in your life or involvement in a variety of programs or community events. Again, the Time-Wasters are not always bad, but they are the things that keep you from spending time on the habits necessary for your growth.

When I started SouthHills Community Church in Corona, California, I was heavily involved with another organization led by my good friend Donny Burleson. This organization is called "On Fire" and its purpose is to speak into the lives of teenagers across America through our public school system. On Fire speaks about topics such as peer pressure, making right choices, and living drug and alcohol free. This is a great organization and I was honored to be a part of it, however, when my wife and I began the process of planting a brand new church, this endeavor took much of our time. So much that I was forced to pull back from On Fire. Does that make speaking in schools a bad thing...of course not. It just wasn't the best thing for my life.

That's what you have to do. You have to decide what are the Habits that are necessary for you to achieve your dreams. Then you have to make a list of what activities, good or bad, in your life, need to be removed or even cut back in order to have more time for the Habits that are right for you.

DO AT LEAST ONE THING A DAY YOU DON'T WANT TO DO

There are so many things in our daily routines that we know we need to do but we keep putting off. Making a phone call to someone we don't want to, working on a project that needs to get done, but is not something we enjoy, or maybe facing a confrontation that is inevitable, but we continue to wait just one more day. There are several things we don't like to do, so we simply put them off. Phone calls don't get made, meetings go unscheduled, paperwork piles up, and "to do" items simply get transferred to the next day. There are things that help us succeed, that cause us to do our jobs better and even create growth in our personal lives, but we put these things off and say, "I'll take care of that 'one of these days.'" As you well know, 'one of these days' is none of these days. I read once, "Today is the tomorrow that you said yesterday you would get it done."

I am not someone who likes to waste time, I enjoy productivity. But just like you I am committed to doing certain things everyday of my life. Each morning I wake up, shave, shower, iron my clothes, brush my teeth, comb my hair, and get ready for the day. As silly as this may sound to you, this bores me. I think about the 30-45 minutes per day it takes to accomplish these tasks. The 5.25 hours per week totaling 273 hours per year that I could be doing something else. There are a lot of things in life that are not our most favorite things to do, but we have to do them. I encourage you to develop the "Right Habit" of doing at least one thing per day that you know you need to do, but keep putting off. Do this and it will help you become the person you dream of being.

MAKE SUCCESS A HABIT

My final challenge to you in this pursuit of developing Right Habits is to make "Success" a regular Habit in your life. There is something extraordinary when you can begin to put wins underneath your belt. The wins create a momentum and that momentum becomes the fuel that charges you up the mountain toward Higher Ground. In the 2001 NBA playoffs, the Los Angeles Lakers had won 15 straight games and seemed unstoppable. In the championship series they lost the first game to the Philadelphia 76ers. This was a huge upset for the Lakers and their fans. No one expected them to lose. Everyone had anticipated a sweep by the Lakers. The reason people had gained such confidence in the Lakers is because "Success" had become a Habit for them. They were used to winning and we the fans were used to seeing them win.

That's what the habit of success does. It gives you a confidence and a momentum that makes you unstoppable. I have a picture that hangs in my office that says, "Nothing succeeds like success." That's true! If you want to be successful, discover the power in making success a habit. For you it may be completing certain projects by the end of the month or reaching a financial goal by the end of the year, or getting started and far down the road on something you've said you were going to start but still haven't. If you can do these things and do them with excellence, you will begin to gain a confidence that comes from making success a habit.

As I said in the beginning of this chapter, Habits may possibly be the most important tool for your success. You may not notice the difference right away, but eventually you will. Developing the Right Habits will ultimately lead you to achieve all your dreams and goals. The Right Habits have proven to be the deciding difference between first and second, Gold and Silver, success and failure. Change your habits from what is good to what is best, from what hinders you, to what helps you, and ultimately you will find yourself at a level you once thought impossible!!

7

HIGHER GROUND BECOMES SHAKY GROUND WITHOUT THE BALANCE OF SOLID GROUND

PART 1

Throughout this book I have hopefully been inspiring you and challenging you to continually reach for Higher Ground. I am one who believes in the human spirit, and that everyone is loaded with potential and has the ability to accomplish great things. I believe in people's abilities so much that I have dedicated my life to helping individuals discover the possibilities that lie within each person. However, I must admit that over the years I have met many people that have pursued their personal Higher Ground, and have reached a level of success that many others would desire, but they are not happy. They have a business that's thriving, financial security, and have many personal achievements, but their life still seems to be lacking. Why is that? Why is it that some people seem to have it all, but still seem to have nothing?

Probably because most people connect the word "success"

with the word "money." When you see someone who is financially independent, there is an automatic feeling that the person is successful. There are a lot of enjoyable things that money can buy, but success cannot be limited to these things. Success must include the things money cannot buy. It has been said that money can:

1. Buy a bed, but not sleep,

2. Buy affection but not love,

3. Buy company, but not friends,

4. Buy a wedding, but not a marriage, and

5. Buy a house, but not a home.

I was recently having lunch with a friend who shared with me some sad news regarding a mutual friend. We'll call this friend of mine "Mike." Mike has had a great level of success in many areas of his life. He was not born into a wealthy family, but decided at a young age that he was going to make something of himself. In his early 20s he began working for someone else on the weekends while running a small retail business. Over a few years, this business began to grow in such a way that he was able to quit his weekend job and devote himself entirely to his business. He worked hard, dedicated his time and efforts, and year after year it continued to pay off in great dividends.

He expanded his small shop and began to build his own place. Soon he was operating his business from a 35,000 square foot shop in which he began to see his business hit a new level of success. Over time he diversified into multiple projects including real estate, and each project brought him success. Everything he touched turned to gold. Mike was an entrepreneur and an icon in the city in which he lived. The sad news that was shared with me at lunch was that Mike had been diagnosed with a disease, and his chance for survival slim. As I was told this news regarding my friend, I drove back to my office and began to think about his life. Death always causes you to think about life.

I asked myself, "was Mike a success?" Then I realized, you can't answer that question until you define success. So first I thought about his finances. Undoubtedly he is a success when it comes to money. He is a multi-millionaire and has enjoyed all the things that life has to offer. Vacations, houses, big cars, country clubs, anything he wants he can have. I thought about his career, was he a success? There is no doubt about this either. Mike has lived out the American dream. He did not come from a wealthy or affluent family, but he worked hard, remained dedicated, and his business was and is a thriving success. Then I began to think about his personal life. He had one failed marriage and his current marriage is on the rocks. Mike seemed to have worked so hard to make a living that he had forgotten to make a life.

I began to also think about his children. Each of them have shared in their own personal struggles. Drug abuse, illegitimate children, a low standard of values, and morals are all part of the story behind Mike's children. I am not saying that Mike was a bad parent or that his children don't love him. What I am saying is that, to a certain degree, Mike did not fulfill his parenting obligation by raising his children with a deep level of character. Regarding any spiritual awareness, there has been none in his life and nothing passed on to his children.

Then I thought about the disease that is taking over his body and I couldn't help but wonder what words would be said at his funeral if he should die. I wondered about the legacy and heritage he will leave. Has there been anything done in his life that will outlast him? I thought

> "ALWAYS MAKE SURE YOU HAVE SOMETHING TO GO HOME TO."

about the words of Ralph Waldo Emerson when he spoke of the true picture of success.

"To laugh often and much, to win the respect of intelligent people and the affection of children. To earn the appreciation of honest critics and endure the betrayal of false friends. To appreciate beauty, to find the best in others, to leave this world a bit better, whether by a healthy child, a garden patch or a redeemed social condition. To know even one life has breathed easier because you have lived, this is to have succeeded."

Now that you have a clearer picture of Mike, what do you think? Does the word "money" make him successful?

Don't get me wrong, money is a great thing and can be used for great purposes, but you cannot classify money as the means for success. You see, Mike had a dream. He wanted to create a successful business and make lots of money, and he did. However, one thing Mike forgot to do was to keep his feet on "solid ground" while reaching for Higher Ground. Mike had forgotten the golden rule behind the principle of Higher Ground. The rule is, "Higher Ground becomes Shaky Ground without the balance of Solid Ground."

Consider the courageous people called tightrope walkers. They stand on a thin rope suspended high in the air, and they walk across from one side to the other. The key to the entire success of that tightrope walker is one word…"balance." His entire life is dependant on his ability to keep things in balance. The same is true for anyone seeking Higher Ground. Their entire success is depending on this one word…"balance." Whatever Higher Ground you reach will always be incomplete without balance. Success cannot be limited to financial security, writing a book, starting a business, or even fulfilling a dream. Success is always more than these. I have had the honor to sit and chat with the Chief of Police for the city of Corona, California. His name is Richard Gonzales and he does an

REPUTATION IS WHAT OTHERS THINK YOU ARE, AND CHARACTER IS WHAT YOU REALLY ARE.

outstanding job with our police force. He said that he tells his staff and police officers to "Always make sure you have something to go home to." In other words, he is saying that it does not matter how successful we are in one area of our lives. Success has to contain more than just our careers.

Imagine if you will a large wagon wheel that has various spokes coming out from the center. The ability to make a wheel roll properly lies in the balance. The strength and success of that wheel relies on the spokes being in balance. Let's pretend now that your life is that wheel and the spokes in the wheel represents various areas in your life. These areas include personal, financial, relational, physical, emotional, professional, mental, and spiritual. The success of your life depends on your ability to be successful in each of these areas. In this chapter I want to break down the first four elements for you and provide some practical ideas that will help you raise the bar of excellence in each category. (I will discuss the last four elements in the following chapter.) Remember, the goal is not to say "Well four out of eight ain't bad." The goal is to find yourself pursuing each of these areas and arrive at a new level of success.

❶ PERSONAL

The first spoke in your wheel is the spoke we call "Personal." This is your character, this is who you are when no one is looking. It is the premise of your true success as a person, leader, worker, spouse, parent or friend. Have you ever heard the statement said about someone else, "That person is a real character." They are describing how that person acts whether they are humorous, or fun to be around or maybe they have some interesting trait that makes them unique. But when we say, "That person is a real character" we are usually describing that person's reputation, not their character. Reputation is what others think you are, and character is what you really are. Character is what really matters.

Some people may think character doesn't matter. If it's only what you are when no one is looking, then who cares? It won't affect my business, my family, my finances, nothing will be affected by character because it's who I am when no one is looking. Nothing could be further from the truth! If character doesn't matter, then tell it to the person who just found out their spouse is having a secret affair. Or tell it to the person who just discovered their accountant has been skimming from the top, or that their business partner has left the country with all their money. I promise you this, character matters to those people.

THE AVERAGE SENIOR CITIZEN RETIRES WITH LESS THAN $87 IN THEIR PERSONAL SAVINGS.

Have you ever heard the Boy Scouts Oath? It reads, "On my honor, I will do my best to do my duty to God and my country and obey the Scout Law; to help other people at all times; to keep myself physically strong, mentally awake, and morally straight." Following the Oath, the Boy Scouts repeat the Scouts Motto which is, "Be prepared." and the Scouts Law which is, "A Scout is trustworthy, loyal, helpful, friendly, courteous, kind, obedient, cheerful, thrifty, brave, clean, and reverent." These sound like wonderful things. Unfortunately, I never belonged to the Boy Scouts. It was something that I quite frankly thought was for sissies. I realized how wrong I was later in life and especially when I came across this recent statistic.

In 1995 the Harris poll studied adults who had spent a minimum of five years in the Boy Scouts. Their survey showed that 98% of those who were Boy Scouts for at least five years finished high school; 40% finished college versus 16% of those who were not in Scouting. Thirty-three percent have incomes over $50,000 versus only 17% who were not in Scouting. Other studies showed that 11 of the 12 astronauts, who walked on the moon, were former Boy Scouts and 85% of the graduates of our military academies were former Boy Scouts.

"I'D RATHER HAVE ROSES ON MY TABLE, THEN DIAMONDS AROUND MY NECK."

Living the life of a Boy Scout pays off! Honesty, courtesy, kindness, integrity, loyalty, friendliness, and genuine true character is the premise of the Boy Scouts and ultimately the means for their personal success. Thomas Jefferson once said, "Whenever you are to do a thing, though it can never be known but to yourself, ask yourself how you would act were all the world looking at you, and act accordingly." Remember, there are many things in life that others can take from you, a family, a fortune or even health, but character is the one thing that cannot be taken from you...only you can give it away.

❷ FINANCIAL

The next spoke on your wagon wheel is financial. Finances are a big part of our society and are often used as a measuring stick for where you're at in life. Finances are not everything...but they are something. If you want a home, a car, or to take a nice vacation, finances will be required. If you want to send your child to college, or help them get into their first house, finances will be required. Finances are a great thing and can be of great assistance to you and your family. However, I want you to know that I am not speaking of becoming a millionaire, though I'm sure most of us would not mind, and we already know that finances cannot be the source of true happiness. What I am speaking of is the one word that this entire chapter is about...balance. Bringing a sense of balance to your finances.

If you live in America, you live in a country that is full of opportunity. No other place in the world is like America. To have a nice home, car, a good job, a college education, and a relatively good level of financial security, it is available to anyone who wants it. The problem lies not in opportunity or availability, it lies in the failure of properly managing the finances we are given.

Social Security did a study and showed that the average senior citizen retires with less than $87 in their personal savings. Further studies have shown that the average American family has less then $200 in their personal savings. The average person has seven credit cards and over $6,000 in credit card debt. We spend on average $10 for every $8 we earn, leaving most people consistently in debt. All these facts do not have anything to do with the economy in America, but have everything to do with people not properly managing the finances they do have.

Your Higher Ground may not include finances. It may be to raise wonderful children, to learn a second language, to develop as a leader, or to be the founder of a non-profit organization. Whatever your personal Higher Ground is, you must include the powerful benefit of properly managing your finances. I strongly encourage you to discuss your financial future with an expert. Develop a plan for your future, your retirement, college education, to pay off your home, and any other dream that requires finances. You might be saying, "But I don't make a lot of money." It doesn't take as much as you think. Sit down with a financial planner and you will discover the power of budgeting your finances and consistently investing for your future.

❸ RELATIONAL

We now arrive at the third spoke in the wheel that will help keep your life in balance, your relationships. All the personal success in the world doesn't mean anything if you don't have someone to share it with. Unfortunately, people pursue their personal Higher Ground at the cost of their relationships. Marriages lose their romance, children lose touch with their parents, and families become fragmented under the guidelines of success at any cost. We are a society who is in desperate need of turning our attention to the family. What good does it do to have all the money in the world if your marriage is failing, or to have a thriving and successful business at the price of becoming more of a guardian than a parent?

I find great truth in what Yvonne de Gaulle, wife of the French President, once said, "The presidency is temporary – but the family is permanent." Or what Emma Goldman stated regarding the family, "I'd rather have roses on my table, then diamonds around my neck." These great women, with all their accomplishments and financial security, have realized something that takes others a lifetime to realize, true success is impossible without successful relationships. To have a spouse that you love more each day, to have children to laugh and play with, and to have genuine friends with whom you can share your life with, these are commodities that success cannot live without.

I live in Southern California and life is always moving quickly. I have a business to run, a church to Pastor, children that have a variety of activities, and people that want "a moment" of my time. Just like you, I am extremely busy.

Although we never intend it to, this word called "busyness" robs us of our relationships. It's quite easy to let it happen in your life. Primarily because the things we are busy with are often good things and noble activities. However, these events that fill our calendars, regardless of how wonderful they may be, slowly deteriorate our relationships with others. Those closest to us are left feeling like the "runner up" in a race they never wanted to compete in.

Author Max Lucado wrote some wonderful thoughts on how busyness affects our relationships. Here's a paraphrased version of what he wrote:

"Busyness is an expert in robbing the sparkle and replacing it with the drab. Busyness invented the yawn and put the hum in humdrum. The strategy of busyness is deceptive! With the passing of time he'll infiltrate your heart with fatigue and cover the cross with dust so you will be safely out of the reach of change.

Busyness won't steal your marriage from you. He'll do something far worse, he'll paint it with a familiar coat of drabness. He'll replace evening gowns with bathrobes, nights on the town with evenings in the recliner and romance with routine. He'll scatter the dust of yesterday over the wedding pictures in the hallway until they become a memory of another couple, in another time.

Hence, walks won't be taken, games will go unplayed, hearts will go un-nurtured, opportunities for intimacy will go ignored. All because the poison of busyness has blinded your eyes to the wonder of your spouse."

In the course of my life I have seen people speak with deep regret. Regret for not nurturing their marriage, regret for not spending enough time with their children and regret for not having enough people in their lives they call "friends." Although relationships are only one spoke in your wheel of life, it is an important one. Keep your life in balance by keeping in mind what really matters!

❹ PHYSICAL

I have already spent some time discussing the importance of physical condition in your life, so I will not spend too much time here again. Let me just say that I am by no means the expert on physical condition, but I do try my best to stay in shape and eat right. I have got a long way to go, but I am working on it. One thing I will say is that exercising and eating right does affect your approach and perspective on life. It gives you more energy, boosts your self-confidence, and causes you to embrace and enjoy life at a higher level. Oddly enough I seem to get more done with less hours on the days I work out.

Your personal Higher Ground will be limited by your lack of physical activity. Get active, feel better about yourself, and set a plan of action now! Make it a priority to stay in shape and your overall success will reach new heights. Nothing compares to the confidence you feel when you look in the mirror and you are proud of what you see.

8

HIGHER GROUND BECOMES SHAKY GROUND WITHOUT THE BALANCE OF SOLID GROUND

PART 2

In the previous chapter we began looking at the eight elements that keep our life in balance. We referred to the elements as spokes on a wheel and that in order for the wheel to move quickly and freely it has to be in balance. The eight spokes included:

- **PERSONAL,**

- **FINANCIAL,**

- **RELATIONAL,**

- **PHYSICAL,**

- **EMOTIONAL,**

- **PROFESSIONAL,**

- **MENTAL AND**

- **SPIRITUAL.**

Your Personal Higher Ground is dependent upon your ability to keep these items balanced in your life.

There are some who would argue that these eight elements are an either/or choice. In other words, if you are completely committed to your family life, then you will not have financial success. Or if you are committed to your career, your family will suffer. I couldn't disagree more! I am not one who believes that the eight spokes of life are an either/or choice. I am convicted to believe that all of these things are possible for someone if, they truly work at it and keep it all in balance. I believe with all my heart that each person can live with a high level of character, that their relationships can be rewarding and fulfilling, that they can obtain a comfortable level of financial independence, that they can be emotionally, mentally and physically healthy while maintaining a constant and growing faith in God. Life is not an either/or because Higher Ground does not have to exist in only one area of your life. If you are at least willing to be all that your Creator wants you to be…more and better is always possible.

We have looked at the first four elements or spokes in our life. (Personal, Financial, Relational, and Physical.) Now let's take a look at the final four elements that are necessary to keep your wheel rolling.

❺ EMOTIONAL

We are speaking here primarily of being free of emotional baggage. We live in a society where it is easy to pick up emotional baggage. There are millions of people who are bitter toward a former spouse, angry at a parent who neglected them, have memories of a tragedy that took place in their life, have a friend who hurt or betrayed them or have had a certain event that is causing them to live their lives with constant resentment. This type of baggage is like a giant weight that is attached to your heart, and it keeps you from climbing to Higher Ground.

Anybody who knows me, knows that I always say, "The events in your life can make you 'bitter' or 'better.'" The choice is up to you. Unfortunately, many people choose to walk around in life with a chip on their shoulder. Something or someone has hurt them and they just can't let it go. They hold on to this bitterness or resentment as if by holding on, it will somehow change the outcome. I have learned that resentment is like a boomerang. It keeps coming back and hitting you upside the head. I also have learned that most of the time those whom we are resentful toward don't know it, and quite often don't care.

As I continue to climb up my own Personal Higher Ground, I have had my share of darts thrown at me. People have hurt me in ways I would have never expected. Sometimes things were said by people in whom I had personally invested my life. I can choose to let it make me bitter or I can choose to let it make me better. I choose the latter! I don't want to live with resentment. I realize that my Higher Ground in life will be extremely limited if I cannot learn to let it go. I agree with Lady Margaret Thatcher who once said, "The secret of my success has been in my ability to not waste time with regrets." In the same way the former Prime Minister of Britain does not waste time on regrets, I do not want to waste time with resentment. Sam Ewing once said, "It's wise to remember that anger is just one letter short of danger."

> RESENTMENT IS LIKE A BOOMERANG. IT KEEPS COMING BACK AND HITTING YOU UPSIDE THE HEAD.

Please note that I do not want to minimize any event that has hurt you. In my line of work I meet hundreds of people who have real pain from real situations. I feel for them and I do my best to help them overcome it. I want to do the same for you. If there is resentment, anger or bitterness in your life, you have to deal with it. See a counselor or Pastor, but begin to remove that thing that is wrapped around your heart and won't let you go. If you don't, you are destined to live a life short of your capabilities. You will never reach your Highest Ground because you will be anchored by a weight called resentment and it will inhibit you from climbing to the top. Alexander the Great said, "I have conquered the world, but I cannot conquer my own emotions." Be determined to conquer your emotional baggage or in the end it will conquer you!!

⑥ PROFESSIONAL

Years ago a movie premiered starring Billy Crystal - it was called "City Slickers." The movie centered around a character who was set up to be your typical middle aged man. He had a good job, a wife, two children, and was making descent money. However, he had become bored with his life and bored with his work. His job performance was at such a low level that his boss demanded to approve any decision he would make. For his birthday present his two buddies gave him a gift. It was a two-week adventure in which they would move a herd of cows from Colorado to Texas. (I know what you are thinking, it doesn't sound like much fun.) The movie is great and full of comedy, but at the end of the movie when he sees his wife again, she says to him, "I have been thinking, if you want to quit your job because you are not happy, go ahead, we'll get by." He says to her, "No, I'm not going to quit, I'm just going to do it better."

Maybe you can identify with Billy Crystal's character and the thousands of other Americans who say, "I hate my job." Maybe it's not the job you want or maybe it's a job until you finish schooling or until your business gets off the ground. Either way, it's what you do to make a living and where you probably spend about 1/3 of your life. What you may not realize is that the characteristic of someone who is reaching for Higher Ground is also someone who does the best they can in any situation. Every mountain you climb has its share of obstacles. That's what makes it a mountain. It's your attitude toward the obstacles that will make all the difference in your journey to the top.

Martin Luther, in his commitment to excellence, once said, "If you're a street sweeper, be the best street sweeper you can be." Your occupation may not be what you want at this time, but that is not the point. Your attitude toward your current profession will be the same attitude you carry with you throughout life. If you can't strive for excellence at your current level, there's a good chance that you won't be ready for the next level.

The screen on my laptop went out during the writing of this book. After discovering the cost to repair would be the same as buying a new one, I found myself going from store to store to find the best possible deal. I went into one of the national chains that sells computer equipment. I looked at all the laptops they had on display. Since I had a few questions, I found a man on the aisle behind me stacking equipment on a shelf and I asked the man jokingly, "Are you the laptop man?" Without any expression he said, "Yes." I said, "I have a few questions regarding your laptops on display."

> IF YOU WANT TO CLIMB TO THE TOP, MAKE A SOLID FOOTPRINT WHERE YOU CURRENTLY ARE.

He said to me without any apologies, "I'm kind of busy right now, why don't you find someone else." I am usually quick with a comeback, but this threw me off. I have never had a sales person be so blunt with me, and show such a lack of consideration to me as a customer.

A few things occurred to me as I drove away from the store. First, the salesman must not like his job. He must be one of the thousands of people who would rather be doing anything than what he was currently doing. Second, I felt a little sorry for the guy. He obviously does not understand that it is probably his attitude toward his job that will keep him at the current level. His boss is not likely to promote him. Any businessman that comes into the store is not likely to be impressed

"IF YOU WANT TO MOVE FORWARD, KEEP YOUR HEAD ON STRAIGHT."

with his people skills and possibly offer him a job, and the attitude he has toward his current vocation will most likely be carried out in his life.

If you want to climb to the top, make a solid footprint where you currently are. Let those around you see your great attitude. Let them see that you work hard and strive for excellence in each task. There is always room at the top for those with a great attitude, quality work ethics, and superior people skills. Your approach toward your current profession will determine the outcome of your future profession. Put your promotion in motion by living with this resolve, "Whatever I do...I do my best!"

❼ MENTAL

The next spoke in the wheel of life is "mental." The

mental condition of a person strongly determines the out-come of that person's life. Your personal Higher Ground is more likely to be achieved when it is spearheaded by a healthy mental state of mind.

Doctors, psychologists, and behavioral studies all point to the power found in having a strong and healthy mental approach toward life. Even the Bible indicates that our actions follow our thoughts, and that if someone truly believes, they can overcome the mountains in their lives.

Being mentally healthy means having a strong self-esteem. It means believing in yourself, believing that any-thing is possible. It means thinking on a more positive and optimistic level. It's realizing that nothing good comes out of a negative mental approach. That all hope is removed by the individual, who continues to be pessimistic about their own life and their own surroundings. The legendary come-dian Lucille Ball stated, "One of the things I learned the hard way was that it doesn't pay to get discouraged. Keeping busy and making optimism a way of life can restore your faith in yourself."

"If you want to move forward, keep your head on straight." I have learned that many times in my life and in my personal Higher Ground. The church where I Pastor is in the middle of a building program. After only three years in existence we have purchased property and are raising funds to build. Throughout this project there have been many difficulties. The overseeing and raising of millions of dollars, the interaction with the city, working side by side with a project manager and the variety of twists and turns that this project has taken, just writing it out in this book can seem overwhelming. There have been many times where I could have slipped into negativity, where I could have gotten discouraged and lost hope. But like my good friend Chris Turner told me, "Once you have made a decision to climb a mountain, never, ever look back." There is no hope, no joy, no comfort, and no strength found in taking a negative mental approach.

Martin Seligman, a psychologist at the University of Pennsylvania, has proven that optimists are more successful than equally talented pessimists in business, education, sports, and politics. The Metropolitan Life Company proved this theory by developing the "Seligman Attributional Style Questionnaire." This test is taken by applicants looking for employment, and its purpose is to separate those who are pessimists from those who are optimists. Metropolitan Life has discovered that optimistic people (those who have a healthy mental approach) outsell the pessimist by as much as 50% per year. Same talent and same ability, but different mental outlook.

Recently I took my wife and two children on vacation. We went to Cancun, Mexico for seven days. We had a great time. It's a beautiful place to visit and there is so much to see. On our third day there we went where they offered snorkeling as one of the events to participate in. We had heard there were magnificent fish to see in this small lagoon area and we wanted to see it for ourselves. We rented our equipment and we were ready to go. We marched down to the lagoon ready to explore God's creation. When we arrived, we gave our children, who are ages six and seven, a lesson on how to breathe through the equipment while being under water. After our insightful instructions, we were off. Within minutes my six year old son A.J. began screaming for me. He had managed to swallow some of the salt water that accidentally got into his snorkel. From that point on he did not want to participate anymore. He had determined in his "mind" that he could not do it. For the rest of the day he didn't snorkel. A few days later in our trip we went to another tourist sight and found an even greater place to snorkel. We begged him to try and after much per-suading, he finally gave in. He loved it! He snorkeled for hours and saw first hand the incredible sea life of Cancun, Mexico.

I tell you this story to point out a few observations. First of all, my son got it in his mind that a tragedy had taken place. He swallowed sea water. This event shook him up so much that he refused to participate anymore. Secondly, he kept telling me over and over, "I can't do it, I don't know how." He had mentally set in his mind that he was unable to accomplish the task. Thirdly, once he got over it in his mind, he realized that he could do it and the result was an experience he will never forget. You see, this little illustration describes our mental approach many times in our lives. Once we get it in our head that we can't do something, it's very difficult to get past it. Our mind is a powerful thing. When we finally attempt what we once thought was impossible, we realize how much we would have missed, had we continued with our pessimistic approach. Focus your mind on the possibilities, and your mind will direct you to a Higher Ground.

❽ SPIRITUAL

The final spoke in the wheel of life is Spiritual. For those who have a practicing faith, this is what you may call a no-brainer. You have a faith that is lived out each day and you have come to understand the great joy and fulfillment that comes from having God in your life. But for those who have not yet consecrated their life to God or who have put their faith into action, this act of spirituality may seem irrelevant. It may be hard for you to imagine why a spiritual pursuit would be necessary for success. How does God fit into my relationships, career, finances or any other dream or goal I am pursuing?

A variety of studies have been done indicating that having an active faith is helpful for one's day to day life. For instance, Harvard University studied the causes that prayer has on someone's life and discovered that those who make prayer a daily practice are more likely to be healthier and happier. They also did a study indicating those who practice their faith in God have a much greater chance of making their marriage work. The odds of divorce in America is one out of three. The odds for those who have an active faith in God are one out of 1,000. Another study indicated those who practice their faith have a lower level of stress in their lives. Many studies and many facts prove the same that a Spiritual life makes a difference.

I was once asked what difference could God make in my life. I told the person that you can have a great marriage, be relatively successful, and do well financially without God in your life. But the difference between having God and not having God is like color T.V. and a black and white T.V. Both give the same picture, but one is more beautiful, colorful, and richer looking...that is the kind of difference God makes.

I would encourage you, if you do not have a practicing faith in God, to investigate it for yourself. Find a local church who believes in the Lord and the Bible and begin to seek out what it really means. You will discover what millions of businessmen, political leaders, firemen, policeman, entrepreneurs, and small and big business leaders have discovered for themselves...God makes a difference.

PUTTING IT ALL TOGETHER

Before you move any further, think back over all eight spokes in the wheel of life. (Personal, Financial, Relationships, Physical, Emotional, Professional, Mental, and Spiritual.) Think about the ones that you need to work on the most. What needs to change in your life? What priorities are out of line? Are there character issues that need to be handled or maybe some relationships that need nurturing? Maybe you have some emotional issues that need tending or possibly you need a boost of self-confidence and a new positive outlook to help you reach your Higher Ground. Whichever one, or more, it is, begin working on it. Don't neglect one or the other, pursue excellence in each area. Remember the spokes only move smoothly toward the top when they are all in balance. I said earlier in this chapter that the eight spokes in the wheel of life are not an either/or decision. As Zig Ziglar says, "You can have all the things money can't buy and some of the things money can buy," if you will learn to keep it all in balance. Work hard at all eight spokes and become the person you are meant to be!!

9

WHEN IT'S SCARY...
DON'T LOOK DOWN

During the writing of this book so much has taken place in our great nation. It was only two weeks ago (as I am writing this chapter) that our nation faced one of the greatest tragedies in history. It took place on September 11, 2001. A date that no American will ever forget. It was in the early hours of what seemed to be a typical Tuesday morning. People in New York and at the Nation's Pentagon were just beginning their workday, never imagining that today would be their last. There were thousands of people in both locations working hundreds of miles apart, but working together. At the Pentagon they worked each day for our Nation's Security and at the World Trade Center they worked collectively in the buildings that have become an icon for our Nation's Economy.

They were not just employees of a company, they were citizens of a Great Nation. They were moms, dads, brothers, sisters, parents to their children and children to their own parents. They were friends to many and fellow Americans to millions.

I remember watching the tragedy on T.V. Watching the first tower at the World Trade Center hit by an American commercial plane. At first it seemed as though it was an accident. Maybe something had gone wrong with the plane or the pilot, it was a tragedy, but still an accident. Then the second plane hit the other tower of the World Trade Center and all of America knew this was no accident, this was a planned effort by a group of Terrorists against our country. It was followed by another plane that hit our Nation's Pentagon and still another plane that never made it to it's target, but was diverted by passengers aboard the plane (American heroes) and driven into the ground. In the end, thousands of people on board and in the buildings lost their lives. Tens of thousands of people lost their loved ones and millions of people were left with a memory they will never forget.

As I said earlier, I am writing this chapter two weeks after the tragedy. These past two weeks have been a roller coaster of emotions for the American people dealing with the tragedy of the loss of thousands of fellow citizens and watching the economy being drastically affected. Many feel like the foundations of Peace and Prosperity are radically shaken. The airlines are laying off thousands of employees because of a lack of business. People are afraid to fly! We are watching our nation's leaders deciding how to handle the terrorist groups, and we are left wondering is it a matter of "if" or "when" we will be attacked again.

All eyes are glued to the President and his actions from this point forward. People are tuning in their televisions to hear the President's every word. His approval ratings have reached a history high of 90%. People are enjoying what they see. The President has displayed great leadership in the face of danger and uncertainty. He has been optimistic about our nation, he has rallied people to a love for this country and a unity among one another. He has promised to work hard to end terrorism and is acting swiftly, carefully and with wisdom. He has surrounded himself with great counsel and is genuinely working for the American people. He is being a servant to the public in a way this nation hasn't seen in many years.

There is one characteristic that seems to stand out more then any other from our President. A characteristic that has shown itself in many ways and hopefully will continue to show itself in the years to come. I am talking about the incredible attribute called "COURAGE." President Bush has displayed great courage in the face of terrorism and in the face of a country whose foundation has been shaken to the very core. His courage is what will cause this country to rebound, to be stronger than ever before and to restore Freedom, Peace, and Prosperity to this great land that millions call home.

There are many lessons to be learned from individuals

throughout history who have displayed great courage. From the forefathers who founded this country as, "One nation under God," they had courage. To the many men and women in the armed forces who have given their lives for their country, they have had courage. For the Firefighters and Police Officers who have given their lives to protect and serve others, they have had courage. For entre-preneurs, dreamers, and inventors who have shaped our country's free enterprise, they have had courage. For the great leaders our nation has and have had in the past, they have had courage.

> FOR ANYONE WHO HAS A PERSONAL HIGHER GROUND, COURAGE IS NOT AN OPTION, IT IS A MUST.

Courage is a great thing! For anyone who has a person-al Higher Ground, courage is not an option, it is a must. Whatever mountain you are climbing, whatever dream you are dreaming, courage must be something that is placed in your backpack as you journey up to this place we have called Higher Ground. Courage is what causes you to blast through the obstacles and opposition you will face. Courage keeps you going when nothing else will. It is the antidote to your fear and the prescription to your insecuri-ties. Your success in life will be marked by the amount of courage you have. Without courage this country does not have freedom. Without courage this nation does not have peace. Without courage electricity would not have been discovered, cars would not be driven, and airplanes would be a word that would only be foreign to you and me. Without courage television would not have been made, Disneyland would have never existed, companies would have never began, and a man would have never walked on the moon. Courage built our country and it will build your dreams and help you reach Higher Ground.

In my own life, Courage is what has kept me going when facing different obstacles and pressures. Many times fear grips my heart and uncertainty of the future causes me to doubt, but it is Courage that keeps me going. Courage at the very core is always the same. What I mean is that it does not matter who you are or what dream you are attempting to live out, there is a kind of Courage that is necessary for everyone. The kind of Courage I am speaking about is the same kind necessary to be the President of the United States in times of crisis. The same kind of Courage that an owner of a company must have when facing difficulty. The same kind of Courage necessary for

"GOOD THINGS COME TO THOSE WHO WAIT, BUT ONLY WHAT'S LEFT OVER BY THOSE WHO HUSTLE."

you to reach your highest potential or for you to make a dream a reality. Let me break it down for you and show you how Courage is lived out for someone like you who is seeking Higher Ground.

❶ COURAGE TO KEEP CLIMBING WHEN YOU CAN'T SEE THE ROAD IN FRONT OF YOU

As I have mentioned before, the church where I Pastor is in the middle of a building project. Anyone who has been part of any building project knows that there are several challenges that are faced each day. One of the greatest challenges is finances. A great deal of money is necessary to buy the land and to build. A church is a non-profit organization so raising funds can become very difficult. Finding lenders who will finance your project can become extremely difficult.

There have been many times that we have continued our journey even though we could not see the road in front of us. Hiring architects and engineers before we owned the land, because we knew that for various reasons we needed to move quickly. Moving forward with our permit process without having all the financing in place. The list goes on and on of various times in which the road was unclear, but we needed to move forward. That's where Courage comes in. Courage to move forward even when things are a little unclear. Most people make the mistake of waiting until there is no risk involved before they proceed. They create the largest safety net possible and wait for all questions to be answered before continuing their journey up the mountain. I agree with President Lincoln when he said, "Good things come to those who wait, but only what's left over by those who hustle."

Nothing great has been accomplished and nothing wonderful has been invented without the Courage to move forward when the road was unsure. Think of it like driving home at night. You do not get in the car and say I am not heading home until I can see the entire road. You get in your car and you can only see as far as your headlights. (Maybe 30-40 feet.) When you drive the distance your headlights can reach, you continue to drive because now you can see another 30-40 feet. You would never make it home if you waited until the road was clear. The same principle applies for your personal Higher Ground adventure. You will never see the road that leads you to the top! You climb as far as you can go and when it is unclear, you keep climbing. It was Mark Twain who said, "Courage is resistance to fear, mastery of fear – not absence of fear." Everyone gets afraid, but few move forward in spite of their fear. Don't let fear own you or control your destiny, stand with courage, even when you are afraid and keep marching upward!

❷ COURAGE TO MAKE TOUGH DECISIONS

Every great leader, dreamer, inventor, founder or Higher Ground seeker has to have the courage to make the tough decisions. Sometimes we are blessed with the luxury of waiting, contemplating, and seeking advice. Other times the decision must be made immediately and you have to have the courage to make it. That is not an easy thing to do, because no one wants to be wrong. However, the reality is decision making is part of the process for anyone who is on the road to Higher Ground. It has been recorded that former President Eisenhower nearly blew it on D-Day because of his fear to make a tough decision immediately. Before his decision to react he was quoted as saying, "No matter what the weather looks like, we have to go ahead now. Waiting any longer could be even more dangerous. So let's move it!" He proved himself a great leader when he made the toughest decision in his military career and he made it quickly.

Throughout my life there have been tough decisions that had to be made. Sometimes I was right but often I have been wrong. That's part of decision making, you gather the information you can, seek the advice that's available, and you make the decision with courage. I have found that the right decision can become wrong when it is made too late.

Edmund C. Lynch, the founding partner of Merrill Lynch, said, "If I made a decision fast, I was right 60% of the time. If I made a decision carefully, I'd be right 70% of the time, but it was always worth it." You are not always going to be right. When you are wrong, admit it.

VALUES MUST BE STATED AND PLACED FIRMLY INTO THE FIBER OF YOUR PERSONAL AND BUSINESS LIFE.

Correct it if possible and move forward, but do not be afraid to make the next tough decision that comes your way. T. Boone Pickens once said, "Be willing to make decisions. That's the most important quality in a good leader. Don't fall victim to what I call the 'ready, aim-aim-aim-aim syndrome.' You must be willing to fire."

Years ago, I was put in one of those situations where I had to make a tough decision. The decision centered around the standards that need to be lived out by my staff and leaders. As I shared these guidelines with my staff and leaders, it was received well by most, however, there were one or two individuals who struggled with the guidelines. They met with me and shared their opinions, but I knew in my heart the decision I made was the right one. Looking back on it. I would have made the same decision, but I would have approached it differently. Unfortunately, one of the individuals left my leadership and the organization as a whole. I deeply regret this person's decision because I care for them and enjoyed their contribution to the team.

Tough decisions are part of being a leader and part of the journey toward Higher Ground. Bill Marriott Sr. expressed his view of decision making by saying, "Men grow making decisions and assuming the responsibilities for them." Be willing to admit when you are wrong, but never lack the courage to make the tough decision.

David Mahoney said that the worst mistakes he ever made were because of the decisions he failed to make. In 1966 he was the head of Canada Dry. The stock was selling at a low price of $11 per share and with about 2.5 million shares outstanding, he could have bought the entire company for $30 million. About twenty years later, he would have been worth about $700 million. The decisions a person seeking Higher Ground has to make will include:

- **FINANCIAL,**

- **PERSONAL,**

- **STAFFING,**

- **VISION,**

- **MISSION,**

- **HIRING,**

- **FIRING,**

- **RISK TAKING,**

...and the list goes on.

You gather the information possible, seek advice when available, but don't be afraid to make the decision necessary. Courage to make the tough call will quickly mark you as a leader or follower, it will separate you from being a dreamer to being a doer, from a mountain observer to a mountain climber.

❸ COURAGE TO LIVE BY A SET OF VALUES

What are values? Values are the set of standards and guidelines that shape your life. It sets in motion your character, your beliefs, what you will, and will not do. Values are a compass for our life and dictate to us how we live and function in our personal and business life. For anyone who is truly committed to excellence and to live to their fullest potential, values must be stated and placed firmly into the fiber of your personal and business life.

As I began my journey in starting a church from scratch, I had to make sure I knew what the "Core Values" were of this church. Once we established these "Core Values" they became a guide for us. Everything we do is based on these values. If there is a project that comes along but does not add to our existing values, we don't do it. The project may be a great one, but if does not fulfill our values, then we simply don't do it. Over the years my life seems to get busier and busier. As a founder of a church, a public speaker, author, husband, and father my schedule seems to fill up quickly. However, my schedule is guided by a set of values. As I am presented with various opportunities and projects, I have to ask myself, "Will this fulfill my values?" For instance, I was recently asked to speak at a camp for teenagers. I value my time so I had to see if in light of my other responsibilities, I was available. I value my church and my speaking organization so I have to ask, "Will it fulfill my values? Will it add to my goals?" My answer to the person asking me to speak was "no." It wasn't that I didn't see it as a valuable event, it was simply that it did not add to my value or purpose for my life at this time.

You see, that's the value of values...they guide your life and help you make decisions.

Years ago you may remember the scare that took place with Tylenol aspirin. Some of the bottles had been tampered with and they were unsure how many or the specific cause. The CEO of the Tylenol Company made an executive decision. They pulled all the Tylenol bottles from the shelves across America. It was a record multi-million dollar loss. In an interview, the CEO was asked, "How could you make such a quick decision?" "It was easy," he said, "all we had to do is look at our Core Values and that made the decision for me."

The values for each person may vary. Let me share a few values that I hold close to my heart that serve as a guide for my life:

- **GOD** – I value my relationship with the Lord. I do not want to do anything or be a part of anything that will negatively affect my personal relationship with Him.

- **FAMILY** – My family is important to me. I value my wife and my children and I do not allow anyone or anything to tear me away from my relationship and time with them.

- **CHURCH** – The church I started is very important to me. I do not allow projects or events to take away my time or my focus on building this great church.

- **TIME** – I try to guard my time carefully. I do not like to waste time.

- **HARD WORK** – I value hard work. I believe that you get out of life what you put into it. Work hard and life will deal you a good hand.

- **LEARNING** – I am a learner. Reading books, listening to tapes, and attending conferences is a part of my weekly routine. I value the learning process.

- **LEADERSHIP** – Developing as a leader and developing leaders around me is very important. I believe the greatness of any organization falls on the shoulders of it's leaders.

This is just a partial list of the things I value. These things are a compass for my life, guiding me toward what I want to accomplish and what I want to become. It takes "Courage" to lay out your values but even more courage to live by them. If you are going to be a person who truly seeks Higher Ground in your life, you will need values. You will need the Courage to create them and to live by them.

A survey was taken entitled, "The Day America Told the Truth." The question asked in a private pole was, "What would you do for $10 million dollars?" One out of four respondents would abandon their families, 23% said they would become a prostitute for a week, 16% noted they would leave their spouse, and 3% confided they would put their children up for adoption. It is one thing to say something is important in your life and it is an entirely different thing to live by it.

As I stated earlier in this chapter, courage is what this country was founded on and what makes this country great. Inventors and dreamers are people who had the courage to stick it out. Entrepreneurs are individuals who found courage in the face of uncertainty. Courage is what helps to make a couple celebrate a Golden anniversary, what makes a student finish college, and what makes small business owners a success. Whatever your personal Higher Ground may be, decide that courage will be a characteristic you will not live without. Find the courage to keep climbing when you can't see the road in front of you. Find the courage to make the tough decisions that are inevitably coming your way. Find the time to create your own list of personal values and, most importantly, the courage to live them out. Let courage be your ally as you face each day on the mountain.

When it's scary...don't look down

10

YOUR FINAL CLIMBING INSTRUCTIONS

We now arrive at our final chapter in this book. I hope you have enjoyed reading it as much as I have enjoyed writing it. If you have gotten this far, you are in the top 15% of America. Approximately 85% of people who purchase self-help books never finish them. You are in a class by yourself and you are on your way to Higher Ground. Whatever your dreams and goals are, you are more than capable of doing it. You have what it takes!

A while back I took my entire staff to Six Flags Magic Mountain in Southern California. It was a great day, extremely hot, but still a great day! We enjoyed laughing with one another, kidding around with each other, and bonding as fellow staff members. If you're a leader, never underestimate the advantages of spending time away from the office with your staff. Our day at Magic Mountain was filled with rides, jokes, and plenty of food.

One of the rides that were being featured at the time was

called the "Dive Devil." This ride was in the park but you paid separately for it. The idea was that anywhere from one to three people would strap a vest around themselves. You then laid down flat on the ground and you were hooked to a cable that was also attached to an apparatus 15 stories in the air. Once you were hooked onto the cable, you were then lifted in the air to the top. When you pulled the handle, you were released and you would swing down 15 stories and back up the other side in a sort of one-half circle shape. It was like being on a play ground swing, but 15 stories high and lying straight out in a Superman position. It was scary, but lots of fun!

I went on it with two of my staff members, Marv and Sonya. Marv was pretty relaxed, I was a little intense, and Sonya was completely nervous. Probably what made us the most nervous was how quickly they gave us instructions. Within two minutes they strapped us in the vest, and gave us the instructions on what to do, and what not to do. As we were lifting into the air, they were still giving us instructions. We had a great time, but the lack of instructions made us nervous. I learned something that day, that if you have the proper instructions, it helps alleviate anxiety. The more you know, the better you are equipped to face the challenge. That's what I want to do for you in this chapter. To give you some final instructions as you face your personal Higher Ground experience!

Regardless of what mountain you are setting out to

climb, you are going to be faced with challenges. Everyone who has done anything significant with their life or dreams have had their share of challenges. The challenges may vary in size, shape, and appearance, but the root of these challenges is typically the same. Let me give you some final facts and instructions to always remember as you face your personal Higher Ground.

LIFE LESSONS FOR ALL HIGHER GROUND SEEKERS

LESSON 1 The climb isn't always perfect

No road worth climbing is perfect. No worthwhile task is ever easy. If it were easy, everyone would be doing it. Marriage has its challenges, but it's a great experience. Parenting has its difficulties, but there's nothing like the love from a child. Standing in front of a crowd and receiving a degree is wonderful, but it is preceded by hard work and a variety of challenges. The freedom that comes from owning your own successful business is terrific, but it does not come without its share of problems. Any Higher Ground goal you have for your life will have its share of problems.

I have been privileged to be a part of wonderful projects in my life. Some have failed, some have succeeded, but all have had their challenges. The climb has never been perfect for me or for anyone I know. The problem is that many individuals start off with good intentions of reaching their goals, but they give up too quickly. Hershel Walker, the famous NFL running back, said, "My God given talent is my ability to stick with something longer than anyone else." That's what it takes to achieve your desires. You must be willing to work hard and stick it out. It is not necessarily your talent or ability that gets you to the top, it is your tenacious spirit that never gives up. I have found that people tend to give up early in the climb for one of two reasons:

> IT IS NOT NECESSARILY YOUR TALENT OR ABILITY THAT GETS YOU TO THE TOP, IT IS YOUR TENACIOUS SPIRIT THAT NEVER GIVES UP.

❶ FEAR

I have talked about this before, but it bears repeating that fear keeps us from climbing. Fear of the unknown, fear of failure, and/or fear of what others may say or think. Fear of not having enough talent, ability or education. Fear attacks our minds, grips our heart, and chokes potential from our life. Fear is a funny thing. It's being afraid of something that has not happened and has not been proven. It's like a child being afraid of the dark. When my little girl was a toddler, she didn't want me to shut the lights off. I sat down beside her and said, "Close your eyes." She closed them tightly and then I asked, "What do you see?" "Nothing" she said. Then I said, "Open your eyes," she did and then I asked her, "Now how can you be afraid of nothing." Now that sounds like a logical point, unfortunately it didn't work, the light stayed on. As adults, we fear what we cannot see or cannot predict, but we allow this fear to control us like helpless children. Next time you are overcome by fear, remember the words of John L. Mason, "Tell fear to go jump in the lake."

❷ FAILURE

Another reason people give up on the climb to the top is because of failure. Something didn't go right, a plan fell through, and rather then pick ourselves up and continue climbing, we throw in the towel and let failure get the best of us. Charles Goodyear purchased an Indian rubber life preserver out of curiosity. He began to experiment with the idea of making a weatherproof type of rubber. It was a known fact that the rubber would become hard as stone in the cold weather or melt in the hot weather.

Mr. Goodyear sank all his money into experimenting with this rubber. For five years he worked at this project. In fact, his family sacrificed their standard of living because of Mr. Goodyear's obsession with his experiment. Finally, after thousands of dollars and countless hours, his experiment worked. He figured out a way to make a weatherproof rubber. Out of humiliation, hardship and defeat, Charles Goodyear won. He turned failure into success and defeat into victory all because he wouldn't allow failure to be the final answer in his life.

LESSON 2 Your climbing companions may let you down

There is nothing like the joy of having people climb with you on your way to the top. I have dedicated an entire chapter to this concept, and I have dedicated my life to help others succeed and to be climbing companions with me. There is such a joy to journey with others, to experience the ups and downs of life with people who share a common purpose with you. Over the years I have been honored to partner with incredible people. I have brought out the best in them and they have brought out the best in me. I love working with my staff, being their friends, partners in purpose, and being each other's greatest fans. However, the reality is that along the way people are going to hurt you. There are people that you will pour your life into and they will, in the end, bring pain to your heart.

There are people on the path to the journey toward the top that will inevitably let you down. Sometimes, through forgiveness and the ability to accept each other's differences, the relationship is repairable and you can continue to climb side by side. Other situations you will find that the person can no longer be your climbing companion. Although forgiveness is a path you must take to continue, the partnership is simply not possible.

> PEOPLE WILL LET YOU DOWN...BUT NEVER STOP BELIEVING IN OTHERS AND NEVER DETERMINE THAT YOUR JOURNEY WILL BE BETTER IF TRAVELED ALONE.

Realizing that people will let you down, you must determine before you ever journey to the top that your faith in the human spirit will not be shaken. You cannot allow yourself to ever become isolated, because part of the joy in your journey is partnership, and sharing the experience with others! You cannot determine that because people let you down, that you must do it all yourself. When someone attempts to do it all themselves, they limit their effectiveness. You cannot accomplish more work with less people, and in addition you will rob yourself of the joy that's found in helping others succeed. Finally, because people will let you down, you will be tempted to doubt others. You will begin to feel that people cannot be trusted. The result will be that your relationships with other climbing companions will always be limited because the shadow of doubt in the human spirit will be lingering in your heart. People will let you down...but never stop believing in others and never determine that your journey will be better if traveled alone. Take others with you and soar your way to the top.

LESSON 3 Enjoy the scenery

My good friend Wes Beavis once said to me, "Chris, remember that the path you are on is a Marathon not a Sprint, it is a Journey not a Destination." He was encouraging me at a time in my life where I was so focused on tomorrow that I was not enjoying today. I must admit that I fall into this trap quite often. I will find myself so focused on the future, and as soon as the future becomes the present, I focus on the future again. It is a trap that robs me of the joy of life. I must constantly be reminded by those closest to me to keep reaching forward in the race, but don't forget to enjoy it.

Remember, that although we want to obtain our goals to see our dreams become reality and to be known as a Higher Ground climber, we must never become so busy with our futures that we forget the present. There are marriages that need to be nurtured and children who desperately need our attention. There are friendships that need to be cultivated, love that needs to grow, and joy that needs to blossom. Our Creator did not make us to be so over burdened by life that it robs us of the joy of living.

> "NO ONE ON THEIR DEATH BED WISHES THEY HAD SPENT MORE TIME AT THE OFFICE."

I am thankful for my wife and two children, who have a perfect way of lifting me to Higher Ground while keeping my feet on Solid Ground. My wife wants me to succeed, but never allows me to forget what really matters in life. She helps me remember what I always say to others, "No one on their death bed wishes they had spent more time at the office." Let me encourage you to keep reaching for Higher Ground, but never forget to water your own ground - the ground you call home, family, and friends. Water them with your love and affection, and your journey to the top will never lack the joy your life was meant to have.

LESSON 4 **If you keep climbing, eventually you'll make it.**

Life has a way of clearing a path for the Higher Ground seeker. For those who want to be more, do more, see more, and become more, life holds a special door open that leads them to the top. Every person who has accomplished something great or has seen their dreams lived out, has faced their challenges, but has found the timeless truth that if you keep climbing, eventually you'll make it to the top.

Throughout the course of my life I have seen this truth lived out in me. I have watched with my own eyes how a path seems to open up whenever I become determined to reach Higher Ground. The key however is in the phrase "keep climbing." It's the ability to move forward and upward and never ever stop reaching. There is an old Christmas cartoon where the characters sing a song that says, "Put one foot in front of the other and soon you'll be walking out that door." You can

> IF YOU DON'T PUT ONE FOOT IN FRONT OF THE OTHER, IT'S A GUARANTEE THAT YOU WON'T GET ANYWHERE.

change the words for your own inspiration and say, "If I put one foot in front of the other, eventually I'll make it to the top." You might be thinking, "I have been putting one foot in front of the other and it seems I haven't made any progress." Well consider this. If you don't put one foot in front of the other, it's a guarantee that you won't get anywhere. If you're a Higher Ground seeker, your only choice is to march forward and upward...so keep marching!

As I have shared earlier in this book, the church where I Pastor is in the middle of a building project. We have had our shares of ups and downs, but we continue to climb toward our Higher Ground. We have found, as we continue to climb, the path to the top has a way of opening up. We purchased the 6.2 acres in June of 2001 and we immediately began the process of working with the city to obtain the necessary permits. We secured an Architect, Engineer and Project Manager and we were off and running. For anyone who has ever been a part of a building project, you know that it is a roller coaster ride of emotion. Each day brings a new set of challenges and, quite honestly, it can be very frustrating. Part of the frustration is dealing with the city requirements and codes. There are hoops you need to jump through and red tape that must be crossed.

> LIFE HAS A WAY OF OPENING UP A ROAD TO THOSE WHO SEEK HIGHER GROUND.

Through the course of the process we began to feel that our project was not getting the attention it needed. We are in a growing community and the city has numerous projects to work on and everyone wants their project done yesterday. In front of our property there is a street scheduled to meet up with another major street, which leaves our property as the primary corner. This is a great location, but it forces us to rely on other people's schedules. Although the new street is a great asset, it has the potential of holding up our property in numerous ways.

One day I was sitting at my office feeling a little frustrated. We found ourselves waiting on other people's schedules, not feeling that our project was being heard and that our questions were not getting answered. It was at that exact moment that I received a phone call from our Project Manager. He said, "I've got some interesting news for you." I began to think there was something else that was going to be piled on to my day. He said, "Before you bought the property, the original owner had sold approximately 2 acres to the city and that left you with 6.2 acres to purchase. The city bought the 2 acres so that they could bring in the new street. However, the owner of the property and the city itself did not record the grant deed, so in short, you legally own the land that the new street is being built on." As you can imagine I was astonished and immediately two words came to my mind..."Toll Road." Obviously I'm joking (sort of), but this turn of events created quite a stir. That day we received numerous phone calls from the city and other concerned parties. They wanted us to grant over the two acres that really wasn't ours to begin with.

By the end of the day I found myself sitting there with our Project Manager and several city officials talking with us about the situation. Now I knew these two acres weren't ours and it wouldn't help us to try to hold it over their heads because without their approval, our project would never get completed. However, this turn of events gave us an audience with the city that we desperately needed. In that one hour meeting we received in writing that they would finish the street in time, they would bring in the sewer lines, which had become an issue and they would begin to fastrak our project. These are questions that we couldn't seem to get answered and now because of this "trump card" we were holding, our requests were met. Since that time everything has moved along and we are receiving the attention our project needs.

This story is exactly what I'm talking about when I say that life has a way of opening up a road to those who seek Higher Ground. There I was feeling like a small fish in a big pond and a door unexpectedly opened up to me. Now this does not mean that it's been easy. This does not mean the road has been a smooth one and that the climb to Higher Ground has been free of obstacles and challenges. I'm simply saying that if you keep reaching for Higher Ground and continue to put one foot in front of the other, eventually you are going to get where you've wanted to go.

ONE FINAL THOUGHT

I said at the beginning of this book that everyone has a Higher Ground. To start a business, write a book, become a noted speaker, own a home, retire early, learn an instrument or a second language. Everyone has a Higher Ground, a dream that possibly they have never expressed to anyone else. My encouragement to you is to use the tools that have been laid out in this book and begin your climb. Set your course towards the top of the mountain where your dreams have been waiting for you. Brush away the dust of insecurity and fear and wipe away the filth of a failed past and begin to see clearly all that you once thought impossible. It is only then you can breathe life into your dreams! Destiny awaits you, so embrace it with all your might! Stay focused, march forward and never settle. Our personal paths may never cross, but if we set our sights at the top I am confident that we will see each other on Higher Ground.

ABOUT THE AUTHOR:

For information regarding products or services.

Chris Sonksen
2585 S. Main Street
Corona Ca 92882
909-734-4141